Upstream

PRE-INTERMEDIATE B1

WORKBOOK

Student's Book

Virginia Evans - Jenny Dooley

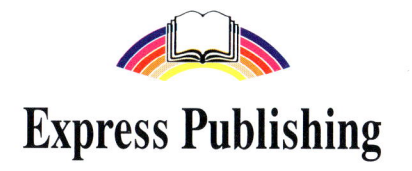

Express Publishing

Published by Express Publishing

Liberty House, New Greenham Park, Newbury,
Berkshire RG19 6HW
Tel.: (0044) 1635 817 363
Fax: (0044) 1635 817 463
e-mail: inquiries@expresspublishing.co.uk
http://www.expresspublishing.co.uk

© Virginia Evans – Jenny Dooley, 2004

Design and Illustration © Express Publishing, 2004

Fourth impression 2007

This book is not meant to be changed in any way.

Made in EU

ISBN 978-1-84558-409-2

All rights reserved. No part of this publication may be reproduced, stored in a retrieval system, or transmitted in any form, or by any means, electronic, photocopying or otherwise, without the prior written permission of the publishers.

Acknowledgements

Authors' Acknowledgements

We would like to thank all the staff at Express Publishing who have contributed their skills to producing this book. Thanks for their support and patience are due in particular to: Megan Lawton (Editor in Chief), Stephanie Smith and Sean Todd (senior editors), Michael Sadler and Andrew Wright (editorial assistants), Richard White (senior production controller), the Express design team, and Kevin Harris, David Smith, Timothy Forster, Steven Gibbs, Eric Simmons and Eric Taylor. We would also like to thank those institutions and teachers who piloted the manuscript, and whose comments and feedback were invaluable in the production of the book.

The authors and publishers wish to thank the following who have kindly given permission for the use of copyright material.

Unit 1: *Who's Who of Giants*, Copyright © 2000-2004 Pearson Education, publishing of Fact Monster, (www.factmonster.com) on p. 8; Unit 2: *Our vehicles* and *Our story* © Innocent, (www.innocentdrinks.co.uk) on p. 16; Unit 4: *Galapagos Highlands & Islands*, © 2000-2004 INCA / International Nature & Cultural Adventures / Inca Floats, Inc., (www.inca1.com) on p. 32; Unit 9: *Donald Duck*, Copyright © 1999-2004 Donald D. Markstein (www.toonopedia.com) on p. 72

While every effort has been made to trace all the copyright holders, if any have been inadvertently overlooked the publishers will be pleased to make the necessary arrangements at the first opportunity.

Contents

UNIT 1	Heroes & Villains	p. 4
UNIT 2	Lifestyles	p. 12
UNIT 3	Earth Calling	p. 20
UNIT 4	Travellers' Tale	p. 28
UNIT 5	On Offer	p. 36
UNIT 6	Happy Days!	p. 44
UNIT 7	Eating out!	p. 52
UNIT 8	Fit for Life	p. 60
UNIT 9	Going out!	p. 68
UNIT 10	Fast Forward	p. 76

Irregular Verbs	p. 84
Tapescripts	p. 85

Heroes & Villains

Vocabulary Practice
Appearance

1 Complete the crossword.

Across

2 Mary Elizabeth Mastrantonio has got long, ... hair.

4 Eddie Murphy has got short black hair and a ....

7 What do you think about Brad Pitt's .... hair?

8 Sylvester Stallone is famous for his .... build.

9 Leonardo Di Caprio has got short, ... hair.

10 Gerard Depardieu has got .... -length hair.

Down

1 Rowan Atkinson's .... nose makes his face look even funnier!

3 Catherine Zeta-Jones has got .... -shaped eyes.

5 Dustin Hoffman is of medium ....

6 Meg Ryan's short, ... blonde hair really suits her.

Crossword answers:
2 across: curly
4 across: moustache
7 across: shiki
8 across: muscular
9 across: blond
10 across: shoulder
1 down: m o (mo...)
3 down: almond
5 down: b(uild)
6 down: straight

4

2 Use words from both the crossword in Ex. 1 and the table below to describe the people in the pictures. Then, describe your classmates.

age	young, middle-aged, elderly, early mid/late 30s (40s, etc)
build	of heavy build, of medium build, slim, muscular, of medium height
hair	short, shoulder-length, long, curly, wavy, blond, dark, straight, bald — long
complexion	dark, pale, fair
special features	a beauty spot, a moustache, a beard, glasses, wrinkles, dimples

Tom

Tom is in his late 40s. He's of medium build, and is bald with a dark complexion. He's got a beard and a moustache.

Sarah

Betty

Ryan

Character adjectives

3 Use the adjectives in the list to complete the exchanges.

- ambitious • lazy • sociable • bossy • selfish
- cheerful • patient

1 A: She's always telling people what to do.
  B: Yes. She's so *bossy*.
2 A: Peter loves going to parties.
  B: I know. He's really *sociable*.
3 A: Sally never thinks about other people!
  B: I agree. She's a very *selfish* girl.
4 A: Is James still in bed?
  B: I'll wake him up. He's a bit *lazy*.
5 A: She wants to be a lawyer one day.
  B: Well, she is a very *ambitious* young lady.
6 A: You're in a good mood.
  B: Yes. I am feeling rather *cheerful* today.
7 A: Aren't you ready yet?
  B: I will be in two minutes. Be *patient*!

Word formation: Nouns into adjectives

We can form adjectives by adding various suffixes to nouns and verbs.
Adjectives ending in **-ful, -ish, -ible, -ous, -ic, -(en)ing** describe sb or sth as having the quality expressed by the noun or verb.
success – successful   child – childish

4 Fill in the blanks with adjectives derived from the word in bold.

1 Be *sensible*! Don't spend all your money on a new car! **SENSE**
2 He received the news with *boyish* enthusiasm. **BOY**
3 Carrie should be more *careful* with her money. **CARE**
4 Fortunately, a *courageous* man jumped into the water and rescued the child. **COURAGE**
5 The climbers had a *frightening* experience on the mountain. **FRIGHTEN**
6 Ireland has a rich *poetic* tradition. **POET**

Adjectives with prepositions

5 Choose the correct preposition.

1 Tamara is worried for/**about** her son's behaviour at school.
2 My boss is very careless **with**/about his belongings.
3 Our English teacher is very popular to/**with** the students.
4 Linda is very sensitive **to**/about other people's needs.
5 Thomas is very clever with/**at** Maths and Chemistry.
6 More and more girls are interested about/**in** computers these days.

1

Grammar in Use

Exploring Grammar: Present simple/continuous

1 a. Read the riddle and try to answer it. Look at the key. Were your guesses correct?

Jay's RIDDLE

1. 10th FLOOR — Jay lives on the 10th floor of a building.
2. GROUND FLOOR — Every day he takes the lift down to the ground floor.
3. When he comes back, he takes the lift up to the 7th floor and then
4. 7th FLOOR — ... he takes the stairs to his apartment on the 10th floor.
5. It's raining today and Jay ...
6. 10th FLOOR — ... is taking the lift straight to the 10th floor.

Why doesn't Jay always take the lift to the 10th floor?

KEY: Jay is short; he can reach the button for the 7th floor. Today he's carrying his umbrella so he can press the button for the 10th floor with it.

b. Read the riddle again and answer the questions.

1 What tense are the verbs in the *first two captions*? What does this tense describe?
2 What tense are the verbs in *captions 5 and 6*? What does this tense describe?
3 What time expressions are used with these two tenses?
4 Put *he takes* (caption 2) in the present continuous. What spelling changes do you notice?

2 Underline the correct tense.

1 A: This week we **are having**/have extra English classes in the afternoons.
   B: Oh no! I can't make it! I usually **have**/am having yoga classes in the afternoons!
2 A: What **do you do**/**are you doing** next weekend?
   B: Well, I **visit**/**am visiting** my family in London.

3 A: What time **does the film start**/is the film starting?
   B: At 8.30! We'd better hurry because it **takes**/is taking a long time to get there.
4 A: Our English teacher **is marking**/marks our projects right now.
   B: Really? I **hope**/am hoping she will give me a good mark.
5 A: What time **are you finishing**/**do you finish** work on weekdays?
   B: Usually around 5 o'clock, but today I **work**/**am working** overtime.

Non-continuous verbs

3 a. Put the verbs in brackets in the *present simple* or *present continuous*.

1 a) I ......think...... (think) about joining a gym.
  b) I ......think...... (think) she's 12 years old.

6

2 a) You ....look........ (look) tired.
   b) Be quiet. The teacher ....look........ (look) at us.
3 a) He ....see........ (see) the doctor tomorrow morning.
   b) I ....see........ (see) what you mean – the room does look bigger with the desk by the window.
4 a) She ....smell........ (smell) the roses.
   b) Their house ....smell........ (smell) of garlic.
5 a) They ....have........ (have) a big garden.
   b) We ....have........ (have) a party next week.

b. How does the meaning of these verbs change in each case?

4 Form questions, then answer them.

1 What / your / is / drink / favourite?
   What is your favourite drink? water
2 What / leave / school / time / do / for / you?
   What time do you leave for school? at 9:00
3 Which / like / most / the / school subject / you / do?
   Which school subject do you like the most?
4 How / you / free / spend / time / do / your?
   How do you spend your free time?
5 What / you / weekend / are / this / doing?
   What are you doing this weekend?

Adverbs of frequency

5 a. Fill in the correct adverb of frequency.

• often • rarely • sometimes
• always • never • usually

always
usually
often
sometimes
rarely
never

b. Use the prompts to write true sentences about yourself and the members of your family. You can use your own ideas.

• play video games (in the afternoon)
• go to the cinema (on Sunday)
• play football (on Saturday)
• help around the house
• watch TV (in the afternoon)
• visit friends (at the weekend)
• do the shopping
• go to bed (early/late)

My father never plays football on Saturday
My mother rarely visit friends at the weekend
I sometimes go to the cinema on Sunday
My brother/sister usually helps around the house
In my family, we often watch TV in the afternoon
I always do the shopping

Phrasal verbs: get

Choose the correct particle.

1 A: Could you get **on/through** the phone to Jack and ask him to come here?
   B: Yes, of course. I'll call him right now.
2 A: She always leaves work early. I don't know what she gets **on/up** to.
   B: Oh, you don't need to worry about her.
3 A: Could I get **off/back** to what I was talking about?
   B: Sure! Sorry I interrupted you.
4 A: Excuse me. How do I get to the post office?
   B: You need to get **off/on** at the next stop and the post office is across the street.

Sentence transformations

7 Complete the second sentence so that it means the same as the first. Use no more than three words.

1 Laura has an appointment with the dentist today.
   Laura is .... dentist today.
2 Describe Bob to me.
   What .... like?
3 Bill still has a cold.
   Bill hasn't .... cold yet.
4 Ann is enjoying herself.
   Ann .... a great time.

7

1

Reading

1 a. Which of these words best describe a giant?

- enormous
- short
- of medium height
- gentle
- weak
- strong
- elegant
- kind
- cruel
- clever

b. Skim the first paragraph and check your answers.

2 Read the whole text and the questions below carefully. Choose the best answer, A, B, C or D.

1 In this text the author is describing
   A different civilisations.
   B real stories.
   C large creatures.
   D fairy tales.

2 According to the text, some giants
   A are not very strong.
   B can be quite nice.
   C are taller than trees.
   D live for a long time.

3 What is the best description, according to the author, of giants in Germanic and Scandinavian tales?
   A They are friendly.
   B They are nasty.
   C They are helpful.
   D They are scary.

4 What have scientists found?
   A large skeletons millions of years old
   B very large bones
   C proof that giants never existed
   D large animals living in the Himalayan mountains

5 The author believes that
   A giants existed a long time ago.
   B it's silly to believe such stories.
   C giants still exist but we haven't seen them.
   D some of the stories may be true.

3 Look up the words in bold and give synonyms for the highlighted words.

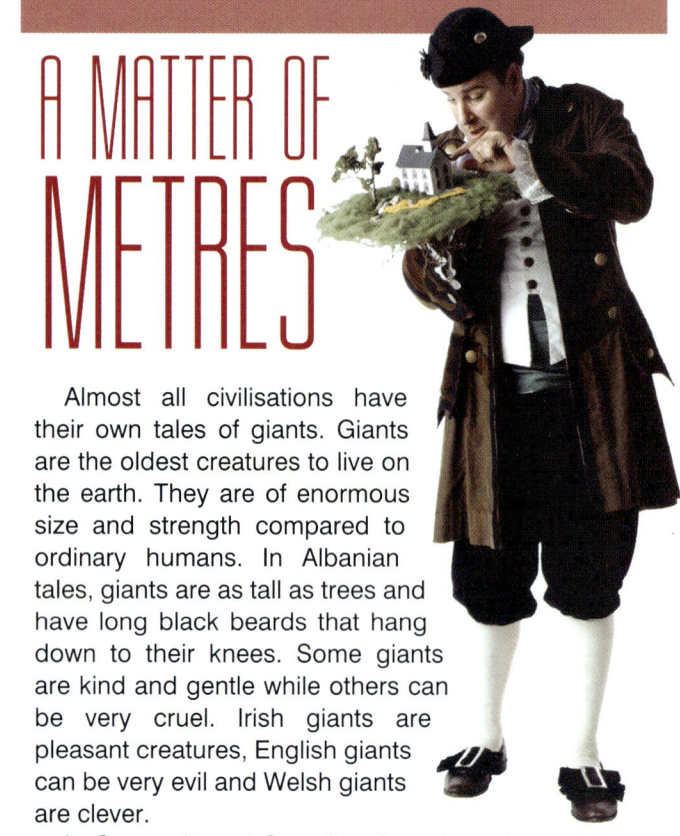

A MATTER OF METRES

Almost all civilisations have their own tales of giants. Giants are the oldest creatures to live on the earth. They are of enormous size and strength compared to ordinary humans. In Albanian tales, giants are as tall as trees and have long black beards that hang down to their knees. Some giants are kind and gentle while others can be very cruel. Irish giants are pleasant creatures, English giants can be very evil and Welsh giants are clever.

In Germanic and Scandinavian tales, giants or trolls can be either friendly and helpful or nasty creatures, but they are always frightening. They can take the form of any animal they choose whenever they like and people believe that they cause storms, hurricanes and even earthquakes. We see them living in castles or under bridges where they force travellers to pay money to pass. American **folk tales** describe how Paul Bunyan, a giant lumberjack who makes lakes and rivers whenever he wishes, creates the Black Hills and the Grand Canyon. He is a symbol of strength and energy.

Are giants simply fairy tale characters? Scientists have found gigantic **skulls** and huge **jaws** which they say belong to giants who were on the earth half a million years ago. Moreover, there are many stories of **sightings** of mysterious giant creatures. Many people believe that there is a giant human-like creature, the Yeti or Abominable Snowman, living somewhere in the Himalayas. Others talk of Bigfoot, a large, dark, **hairy** giant with enormous feet, that lives somewhere in the Canadian **wilderness**. They say it is at least 2.2 metres tall.

Giants fascinate people and appear in many stories, old and new, but the mysteries of certain giants such as the Yeti may be more than just a fairy tale.

4 Can you think of a similar folk tale in your culture? Write a short paragraph about it.

Listening & Speaking
Body language

1 🎧 You will hear someone talking about body language. Read the statements 1-5 and try to guess the correct answer (A-C). Listen and check.

1 We use non-verbal communication when we
   A remain silent.
   B send messages with our body.
   C are interested in others.

2 Non-verbal communication helps us to
   A know how people feel.
   B understand our body better.
   C avoid telling lies.

3 Some people show that they like someone by
   A going far away.
   B standing close to them.
   C talking to them.

4 Body language
   A is common to all cultures.
   B doesn't depend on culture.
   C differs from country to country.

5 Looking into people's eyes
   A shows agreement.
   B shows that you are not interested.
   C is impolite in some cultures.

Socialising

2 Complete the dialogue.

A: Hi there! How are you?
B: 1) ....
A: Not so good, actually.
B: 2) ....
A: Oh, I have a toothache!
B: 3) .... the dentist?
A: Yes, I'll do that. Thanks.
B: Take care. See you tomorrow.
A: 4) ....

Saying goodbye

3 Choose from the phrases (a-g) to complete the exchanges (1-5).

a That's all for now.
b It was a pleasure to meet you.
c Let's get together again.
d Bye! See you later.
e Hope we meet again.
f Looking forward to hearing from you.
g See you tomorrow.

1 A: So, I'll meet you outside the cinema at 7:00.
  B: OK. ....!
2 A: I had great fun at the beach today.
  B: So did I. ....
3 I think .... Write back soon.
4 A: It was a pleasant surprise meeting you today!
  B: Yes, indeed. I ....!
5 A: Well, Mr Williams, it was nice to meet you.
  B: ...., too, Mr Smith.

Personal qualities

4 a. Read the first exchange. Who's angry? Can you guess why?

b. Read and check. Now take roles and continue the dialogue.

Kate: That's it! I've had enough!
Adam: What's the matter, Kate?
Kate: It's Jane – my so-called 'friend' at work. She's so dishonest! She's always telling lies to get me into trouble.
Adam: Really? But she looks so sweet!
Kate: Exactly! Just because she's got big blue eyes and curly blonde hair, everyone thinks she's an angel – but she's not!
Adam: Oh, come on. Don't you think you're being a bit mean? She's always very friendly to me.
Kate: Of course she is. She doesn't want you to see how evil she is. She's always doing terrible things and then telling everyone that it's all my fault! I'm fed up with it!
Adam: Oh dear ... Listen, why don't we go and watch a film after work so you can forget all about her?
Kate: Yeah, OK. What's on?
Adam: Erm ... well, there's a comedy called *Forever Friends* ...
Kate: Oh, perfect!

c. Read again and use the words/phrases in the columns to make as many true statements as possible.

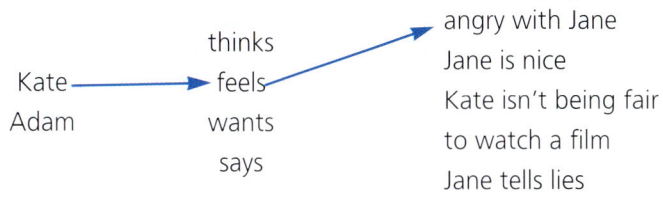

Kate   thinks   angry with Jane
          feels   Jane is nice
Adam   wants   Kate isn't being fair
          says   to watch a film
                      Jane tells lies

Kate feels angry with Jane.

1

Writing (an informal letter)

Getting started

1 Read the rubric and underline the key words (i.e. words which tell you what to write about). What kind of text are you asked to write?

> This is part of a letter you received from an English pen-friend.
>
> *In your next letter, please tell me all about your best friend. What does he/she look like? What is he/she like?*
>
> Write your letter.

2 How would you describe your best friend? Brainstorm according to the key words and complete the mind map.

- looks like (appearance)
- best friend
- clothes
- sports/activities
- is like (character)

Let's look closer

3 Read the letter Tonia wrote and complete the paragraph plan. Which of the two girls in the picture is Tomiko?

Dear Sergio,

1▶ Thank you for your letter. I'm sorry I didn't answer earlier, but I was very busy with my end of term exams.

2▶ In your last letter you asked me about my best friend. Her name's Tomiko and she is quite good-looking. She is 12 years old, with brown eyes and shoulder-length dark hair. The first thing you notice about her is her height! She is quite tall for her age, very slim and fit. She loves wearing casual clothes such as jeans and trainers.

3▶ Tomiko is sociable and outgoing. She loves chatting on the phone with her friends and taking part in team activities, especially sailing and volleyball. Her strongest point is her sense of humour. She manages to make us laugh even in the most difficult situations.

4▶ Tomiko is a very special person who means a lot to me! We may be as different as chalk and cheese, but we are inseparable and nothing is more fun than being together!

5▶ Well, that's all for now. What about your best friend? Write back and tell me all about him!

Love,
Tonia

Introduction
(Para 1) *Opening remarks*

(Para 2) ....
....
....

(Para 3) ....
....
....

(Para 4) ....
....
....

Conclusion
(Para 5) *Closing remarks*

Opening/Closing remarks

4 a) Underline the sentences Tonia uses to start/end her letter.

b) Which sentences could you use to start/end an informal letter? Write *(O)* for opening or *(C)* for closing.

1 Drop me a line as soon as possible. ......
2 That's all my news! I'd better go and do some work now! ......
3 Hi! How's everything going? ......
4 Sorry that I haven't written for ages, but I've been busy studying. ......
5 Please write soon and tell me all your news. ......
6 Drop me a line and tell me all your news. ......
7 Thanks very much for your letter. ......
8 Hi! How are you? ......

1

Linking words and phrases

- When we describe people we can use a variety of linking words and phrases to join sentences together and make our piece of writing more interesting.
  Gerald has got fair hair. He's got blue eyes.
  *Gerald has got fair hair **and** blue eyes.*
  Kelly is a pretty girl. She's got long curly hair.
  *Kelly is a pretty girl **with** long curly hair.*
  Bob is a handsome man. He is in his mid-thirties.
  *Bob is a handsome man **who** is in his mid-thirties.*
  George is tall. He is well-built.
  *George is **both** tall and well-built.*

- When we describe people's character we can include positive and negative qualities. When we talk about negative qualities we should use neutral language.
  *He **seems to** be/**tends to** be/**can** be rather irresponsible at times.*

- Here are some ways we can join sentences:

Similar qualities
  Sue is easygoing. Sue is confident.
  *Sue is easygoing **and (also)** confident.*
  *Sue is easygoing **and** confident **as well**.*

Opposing qualities
  Mark is cheerful. He can be unreliable at times.
  *Mark is cheerful **but** he can be unreliable at times.*
  *Mark is cheerful. **On the other hand/ However,** he tends to be unreliable at times.*

5 Join the sentences using: *and, who, with, both ... and* or *but*.

1 Paul is a tall boy. He's got short straight hair.
2 Sarah is ambitious. She can be impatient at times.
3 Tom has got a beard. He hasn't got a moustache.
4 Peter is a middle-aged man. He is going grey.
5 Lisa is clever. She is beautiful.
6 Carol has got red hair. She has got freckles.
7 Josh is patient. He is reliable.

Build your vocabulary

6 Use the words in the box to form compound adjectives in the following sentences. Which of these adjectives describe character (C)/ appearance (A)?

- eyed • fisted • hearted • looking • minded
- working • aged • mannered

1 They have a beautiful blue-............. baby boy.
2 Jackson is a very polite, well-............. young man.
3 He can't be that young! He looks middle-............. .
4 Most people think that Brad Pitt is a very good-............. man.
5 My son left his books at school again. He is so absent-............. .
6 The ideal person for the job should be ambitious and hard-............. .
7 For Winston, every penny matters. He's very tight-............. .
8 Mary is a warm, generous, kind-............. woman.

Your turn

7 Use the table below to describe your neighbour. Describe his/her appearance, then his/her character.

Useful language
describing people

Appearance: He/She's got ... hair and he/she's short with ... and ... . She usually wears ... . The first thing you notice ... .
Character: He/She is ... . His/Her best quality ... . His/Her strongest point is ... .

8 Read the rubric and underline the key words. Use your answers in Ex. 7, as well as the plan in Ex. 3, to write your letter.

> This is part of a letter you received from an English pen-friend.
>
> *In your next letter, please tell me all about your neighbour. What does he/she look like? What is he/she like?*

Write your letter. (80-100 words)

11

Lifestyles

stressfull azrelaxing reveas interesting ooc creative ndangerous iln boring

Vocabulary Practice

Jobs

1 a. Find six adjectives in the snake.

b. Use the adjectives to complete the sentences, as in the example. Which jobs can you see in the pictures?

1 Bob is a painter.
   His job is very c*reative*.
2 Mrs Lorigan is an accountant.
   Her job is very s ....
3 Jonathan is a firefighter.
   His job is d ....
4 Barry's mother is an art dealer.
   Her job is very i ....
5 Steve is a gardener.
   His job is r ....

Places

2 a. Fill in the blanks with the words below.

- traditional • rush • industrial • quiet
- seaside • busy • local • crowded

My life has changed a lot since I moved here. It's a(n) 1) .... city with lots of noise. I find it difficult to get used to its 2) .... streets, the traffic during 3) .... hour and the 4) .... shops and restaurants. I miss the 5) .... village I come from, with its 6) .... houses, 7) .... streets and cheap 8) .... shops.

b. Write two more adjectives that form collocations with the words below. Use the collocations from 2a & b to write sentences about the place you live in.

city: ....

streets: ....

houses: ....

shops: ....

12

Giving directions

3 The people in sentences 1-4 all live in the same block of flats but they work in different places in the city. Look at the map and then write how they get to work, as in the example.

1 Tamara works at the local library. To get there, she *turns right, goes along Oxford Road, then turns right again into Bridham street. The library is on her left, between the restaurant and the cinema.*

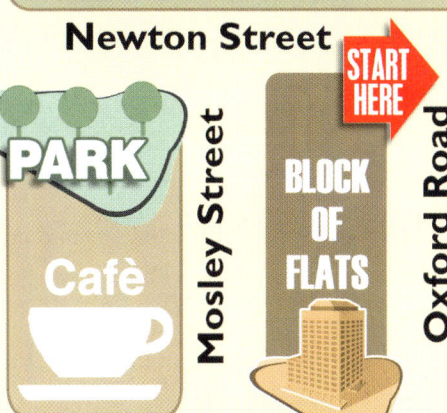

2 Ruth works as a waitress. To get to the café, she ....

3 Georgia works as a teacher. To get to the school, she ....

4 Sergio works for a transport company in the suburbs. He goes there by bus. To get to the bus station, he ....

4 Complete the text with the correct form of the verbs: *take*, *arrive*, *leave*, *travel* and *go*. How do you travel to and from school/work?

Steve usually 1) .... to work by bus. He 2) .... home at 8 am and 3) .... at the office at 9 am. Sometimes, he 4) .... the train to avoid the rush hour traffic. At 5.30 pm he 5) .... the office and 6) .... home on the bus. If the weather is good, he sometimes 7) .... home on foot.

Word formation: antonyms

5 Match the words with their prefixes to form antonyms. Use the antonyms to complete the sentences 1-4.

dis- **in-** **un-** **im-**

experienced mature able honest

1 Jake has never worked on a farm before. He's too .... to run the place by himself.
2 Barry loves playing practical jokes on people. He can be a little .... sometimes.
3 Most people are .... to afford a house with a garden in the city.
4 Paul is .... You can't trust him.

Adjectives with prepositions

*If you are **responsible for** sth you must be sure it gets done.*
*If you are **responsible to** sb you must do what this person tells you to do.*
*You need to be **careful of** sth/sb that/who may be harmful or dangerous to you.*
*You need to be **careful with** sth/sb you may harm or damage.*

6 Fill in: *for*, *of*, *to*, *with*.

1 Mrs Murphy is responsible .... cleaning the offices every day.
2 You need to be careful .... that vase. It's very fragile.
3 Lila is responsible .... Mr Anderson. He is her boss.
4 You have to be careful .... wild animals crossing the road around here.

13

2

Grammar in Use

Exploring grammar: Comparatives & Superlatives

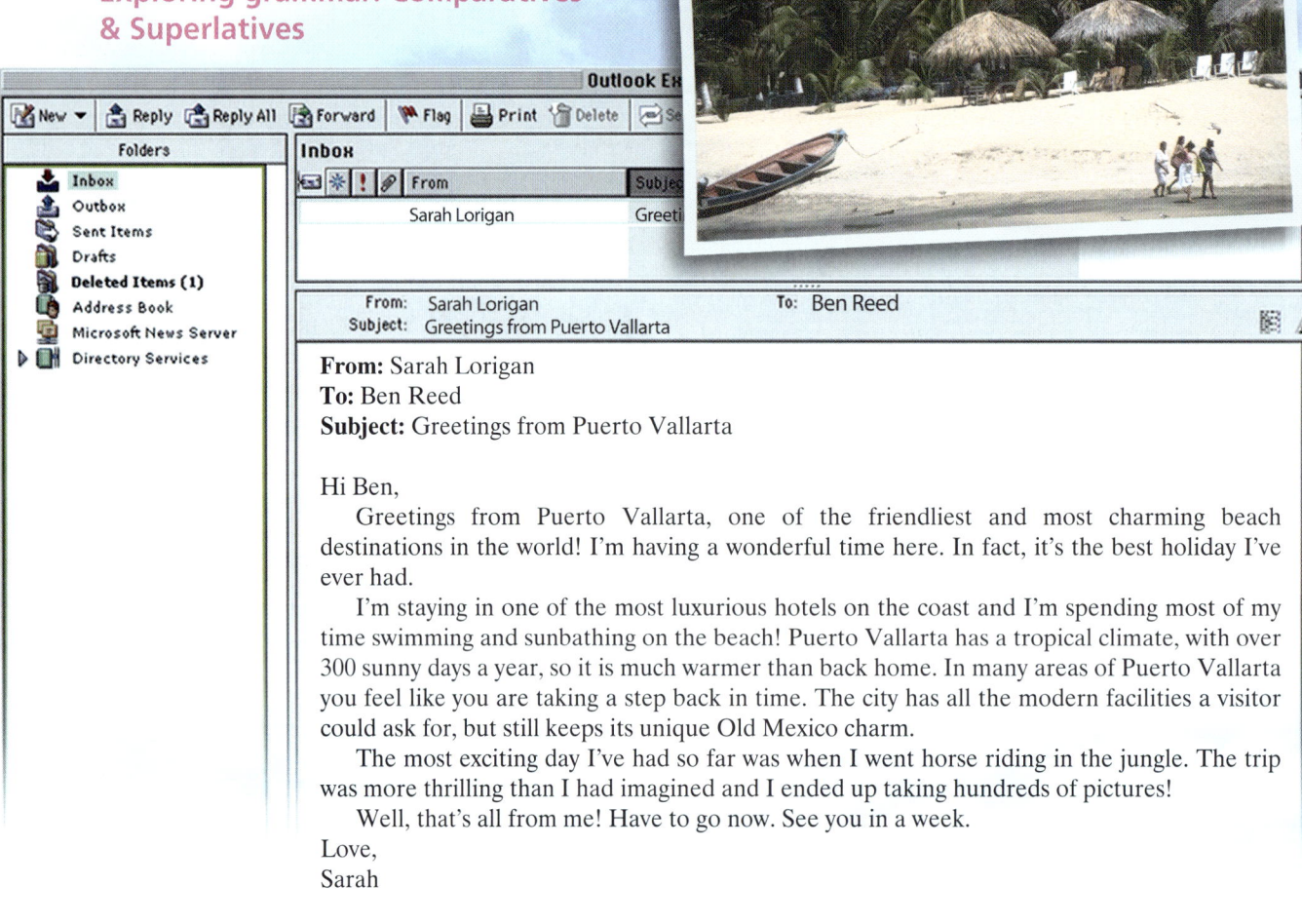

From: Sarah Lorigan
To: Ben Reed
Subject: Greetings from Puerto Vallarta

Hi Ben,
    Greetings from Puerto Vallarta, one of the friendliest and most charming beach destinations in the world! I'm having a wonderful time here. In fact, it's the best holiday I've ever had.
    I'm staying in one of the most luxurious hotels on the coast and I'm spending most of my time swimming and sunbathing on the beach! Puerto Vallarta has a tropical climate, with over 300 sunny days a year, so it is much warmer than back home. In many areas of Puerto Vallarta you feel like you are taking a step back in time. The city has all the modern facilities a visitor could ask for, but still keeps its unique Old Mexico charm.
    The most exciting day I've had so far was when I went horse riding in the jungle. The trip was more thrilling than I had imagined and I ended up taking hundreds of pictures!
    Well, that's all from me! Have to go now. See you in a week.
Love,
Sarah

1
a. Read the email and underline five superlative and two comparative forms.

b. Which endings do we use to form the comparative and superlative of one-syllable adjectives?

c. How do we form the comparative and superlative of adjectives that have more than two syllables?

2 Put the words in brackets in the appropriate form to complete a travel writer's impression of two towns.

Rome and Cervia are two places in Italy with striking differences. First of all, Rome is 1) .... (big) than Cervia. There are 2) .... (large) roads in Rome and 3) .... (many) restaurants, cafés and cinemas than in Cervia. Transport in Rome is 4) .... (good) than in Cervia, but then Cervia has got 5) .... (few) cars and 6) .... (little) traffic. Also, Rome is 7) .... (noisy) and 8) .... (crowded) than Cervia. Rome is the 9) .... (popular) place in Italy. However, Cervia is one of the 10) .... (beautiful) seaside resorts in Italy with some of the 11) .... (clean) beaches.

3 Fill in the correct form of the adjectives, then answer the questions about yourself.

1 What's .... (good) restaurant in your town?
2 What's .... (beautiful) place in your town?
3 Which is .... (busy) street in your town?
4 What's .... (bad) food you've ever eaten?
5 Are you .... (tall) or .... (short) than your best friend?
6 Which is .... (expensive) shop in your area?

14

-ing/to forms

4 a. Read the exchanges and underline the correct words in bold.

1. A: There is no point **trying/to try** to find a parking space in the city centre on a Monday morning, is there?
   B: Absolutely not! It's better **using/to use** public transport.

2. A: I love Edinburgh! You can get anywhere in the city without **to use/using** your car!
   B: I still prefer **to drive/driving** rather than take public transport.

3. A: Don't you find **to go/going** out in a small town rather boring?
   B: Well, I actually don't mind **to spend/spending** time with people I already know.

4. A: I don't enjoy **to eat/eating** in a rush!
   B: I know what you mean. There's nothing I enjoy more than **having/to have** a nice long lunch break.

b. Complete the sentences about the members of your family. Use *-ing* or *to* forms.

My father can't stand ....
My mum prefers ....
My brother/sister hates ....
My aunt/uncle quite likes ....
My grandma/grandpa enjoys ....
My cousin looks forward to ....

Sentence transformations

5 Complete the second sentence so that it means the same as the first. Use no more than three words.

1. His office is bigger than all the others in the building.
   He has .... office in the building.

2. He starts work a lot earlier than his employees do.
   His employees don't start work .... as he does.

3. He likes to go to the gym after work.
   He enjoys .... gym after work.

4. He finds working long hours very tiring.
   He finds it very tiring .... long hours.

Phrasal Verbs: put

6 Choose the correct particle.

1. He's so bossy! I don't know how she puts **on/up** with him.
2. When you finish playing, put your toys **away/out**.
3. Jacques promised to put me **up/away** for a few nights when I'm in Cannes.
4. The pouring rain put us **out/off** going shopping in town this morning.

Error correction

7 Read the letter, find and correct:

- a punctuation mistake (P)
- three grammatical mistakes (G)
- two spelling mistakes (S)
- a case of wrong word use (WW)

Dear Fiona,

Well, here I am in the sunny islands of the Caribbean, enjoying the marvellous weather that is much hoter than in England in the moment. I am in Martinique, the ⟨larger of the⟩ G Windward islands in the, Eastern Caribbean. There is no point to try to call me. My mobile phone is out of order. The sandy beaches are the beautifullest I have ever seen and the food is superb! I can't to stop eating. I've bought lots of souvenirs! My suitcases will be much heavyer because I've bought you so many presents! See you in a week.

Love,

Clara

2 Reading

innocent
little tasty drinks

What is the story behind your idea to start a fruit drinks company, Richard?
We took our fruit **smoothies** to sell at a music festival and put up a sign saying "Do you think we should **give up** our day jobs to make smoothies?" Customers threw their empty juice bottles into either a **bin** marked YES or a bin marked NO. The YES bin filled up so fast that we went into the fruit drink business.

What makes your company different from any other drinks company?
First of all, our fruit and yoghurt drinks are 100% fresh, **natural**, and delicious. We **deliver** daily because they only last about as long as a bottle of fresh milk. Plus, we have a special banana-**shaped** phone in the office that customers call to give us their opinion on our products. We also keep in **direct contact** with all the shops that sell our drinks, from the big supermarket **chains** to the small corner shops.

What about your staff – how do you keep them happy?
We want our employees to enjoy coming to work. Each member of staff gets a **mug** with his or her name on it and all our employees go to lunch together so that they can get to know each other. We also love organising staff weekends where we do fun things like snowboarding.

Why do your delivery vans look like cows?
Well, cows are healthy and natural and so are our drinks, so why not? They even moo instead of beep when you **honk the horn**!

Do you have any advice for anyone who is thinking of starting their own business?
Always listen to your customers, believe in your product and make sure that it is a business you enjoy, because work can be fun.

---

1 Read the title and the questions. What information do they give you about Richard? Who is he? What company has he got? Is he a successful leader? Read through and check.

2 Read the text and choose the correct answer, A, B, C or D.

1 What is the purpose of the interview?
 A to find out how much money the company is making
 B to advertise the fruit drinks the company makes
 C to find out more about the company and why it is successful
 D to make people think about their health

2 How does Richard feel about the drinks he makes?
 A They are tasty and good for your health.
 B They are less important than keeping the staff happy.
 C They are a good way to make money.
 D They are healthier than milk.

3 Why does Richard want customers to phone the company?
 A to find out if they like their jobs
 B to get their advice on starting a new company
 C to get their opinion on the fruit drinks
 D to hear what they think about his employees

4 What does Richard do for his employees?
 A He takes them out for lunch.
 B He makes them feel at home.
 C He lets them run the company.
 D He tells them jokes.

5 Which of the following is the best description of the *Innocent Drinks* company?
 A A Family Business
 B The Future is Here
 C Healthy and Happy
 D Mother Nature's Kitchen

3 Look up the words and expressions in bold, then make sentences with them.

4 Think of other ways of asking the questions in the text.

Listening & Speaking

Describing pictures

1 Look at the picture below and answer the questions.

1. Who do you think the man in the picture is?
2. Where do you think he is?
3. What does he look like? (age, hair, glasses, etc)
4. What is he wearing?
5. What is he doing?
6. What can you see in the background?
7. How do you think he is feeling?

Giving directions/Expressing preferences

2 Circle the correct response, *a* or *b*.

1. A: Do you fancy eating out tonight?
   B: a) I just love Indian food.
      b) I am not hungry. I had dinner at the office.

2. A: Do you want to go to a film on Saturday evening?
   B: a) Not really. I'd rather go to a restaurant.
      b) *The Lord of the Rings* is my favourite film.

3. A: Did you have any trouble finding the office?
   B: a) No, the directions were very clear.
      b) Do you know where the office is?

4. A: Excuse me. How do I get to Prince Street?
   B: a) It's a busy street! There's a huge shopping centre there.
      b) Just go up this road and take the second turning on your right.

Job hunting

3 a. Read the first two exchanges. Where are the people? How are they related? How does Mike like his new position?

John: So, this is your new office. It's fantastic.
Mike: Yeah, it's great, isn't it?
John: Cool! You must be over the moon about getting this promotion. Do you get paid a lot more as well?
Mike: Yes, but to be fair, I work longer hours now, and my new position is more stressful.
John: You know what you need? A secretary!
Mike: That's not a bad idea, actually.
John: I know someone who would be interested.
Mike: Really? Who?
John: You're looking at him!
Mike: What? You? Working for me?
John: Why not? I'm reliable, I'm efficient and I'm your best friend. What more do you want?
Mike: But you're a painter. You don't know anything about being a secretary.
John: Oh well. No harm in asking, I suppose.

b. Read the dialogue. Why isn't John suitable for the job of a secretary?

4 Take roles and give the dialogue in Ex. 3a a different ending.

5 a. Read sentences 1-6. What sort of information do you think the listening passage will give you about Greg and Pam? Discuss in pairs.

b. Listen and mark each statement (✓) *Yes* if it is correct or (✗) *No* if it is incorrect. Were your guesses correct?

		Yes	No
1	Greg hasn't decided what to do after university.	☐	☐
2	Pam has finished medical school.	☐	☐
3	Pam likes some things about her job.	☐	☐
4	Greg thinks that being a doctor is rewarding.	☐	☐
5	Pam thinks being a waitress has good career prospects.	☐	☐
6	Pam doesn't believe Greg is going to become rich.	☐	☐

c. What are your future plans?

17

2 Writing (an email describing the place you live in)

Getting started

1 Read the rubric and underline the key words/phrases. What words/phrases can you think of related to the word 'city'?

This is part of an email you received from your English friend.

> My family and I have just moved to Cambridge. It's green, very peaceful and I like it a lot! What is the city you live in like? Do you enjoy living there?

Now write an email to Helen, telling her what the city you live in is like and if you enjoy living there or not.

Columbus Monument, Barcelona

Let's look closer

2 Read the email and complete the paragraph plan.

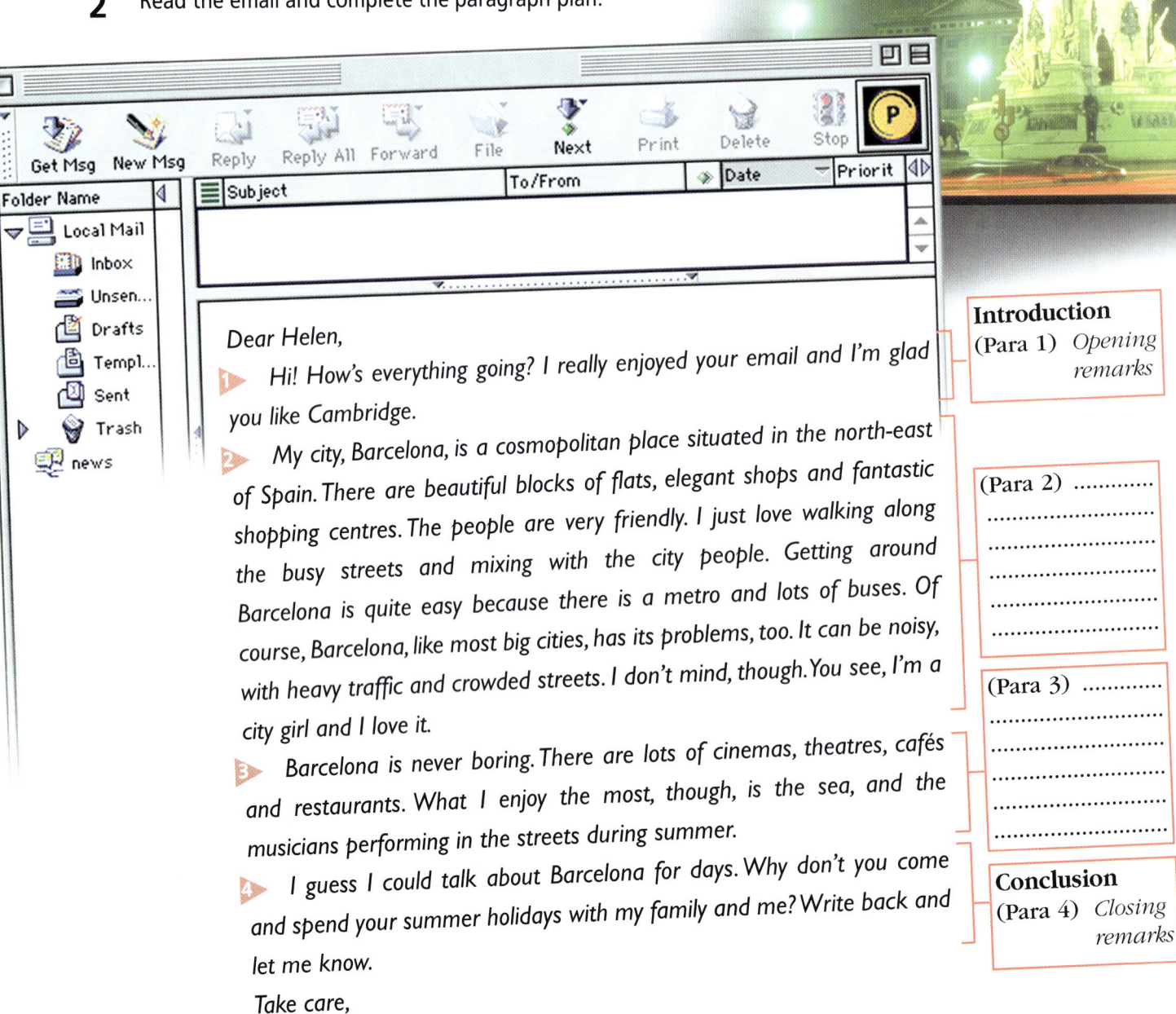

Dear Helen,

1 ▸ Hi! How's everything going? I really enjoyed your email and I'm glad you like Cambridge.

2 ▸ My city, Barcelona, is a cosmopolitan place situated in the north-east of Spain. There are beautiful blocks of flats, elegant shops and fantastic shopping centres. The people are very friendly. I just love walking along the busy streets and mixing with the city people. Getting around Barcelona is quite easy because there is a metro and lots of buses. Of course, Barcelona, like most big cities, has its problems, too. It can be noisy, with heavy traffic and crowded streets. I don't mind, though. You see, I'm a city girl and I love it.

3 ▸ Barcelona is never boring. There are lots of cinemas, theatres, cafés and restaurants. What I enjoy the most, though, is the sea, and the musicians performing in the streets during summer.

4 ▸ I guess I could talk about Barcelona for days. Why don't you come and spend your summer holidays with my family and me? Write back and let me know.

Take care,

Christina

Introduction
(Para 1) *Opening remarks*

(Para 2) ....
....
....
....
....

(Para 3) ....
....
....
....
....

Conclusion
(Para 4) *Closing remarks*

Topic sentences

> The topic sentence is the first sentence in the paragraph. It introduces or summarises the main topic of the paragraph and gives the reader an idea of what the paragraph is going to be about. The rest of the paragraph (supporting sentences) develops the main idea of the topic sentence.

3 Look at the main body paragraphs in the letter in Ex. 2. Underline the topic sentences. Does the information that follows further develop the topic sentences?

4 What do you expect to read in paragraphs starting with the following topic sentences? Can you think of other topic sentences to replace them?

1. Cracow has many impressive sights to see.
2. Nightlife in Moscow is exciting.
3. Cancun is a place that has something to offer everyone.

Using adjectives

> When we describe a place we can use a variety of adjectives to make our description more interesting.

5 a. Complete the table with synonyms from the list, as in the example.

- charming • awful • fantastic • tiny • large
- terrible • huge • enormous • beautiful
- wonderful • horrible • magnificent • little
- elegant

big	large
small	
good/nice	
bad	

b. Replace the words in bold with adjectives from the table in Ex. 5a.

1. Sharon lives in a **very big** detached house in a **nice** suburb.
2. This hotel is really **bad** so you'd better find another one.
3. Pleasantville is a **very small** village situated on the shore of a lake.
4. The view from the hill is **very nice**.
5. The weather is **very bad**.
6. It is a **nice** shop but the service is **very bad**.

Your turn

6 Answer the questions (1-2) about yourself. Use the useful language box.

1. What is your city/town/village like? Think about: location – attractions – shops – transport – nightlife
2. Do you enjoy living there? Why (not)?

Useful language
describing places

location: is situated/is located ... in (the) north/south/east/west/on the north/south/east/west coast of .../in the centre/heart/middle of ...
attractions: fantastic funfair; ancient temples; busy market; sandy beach; medieval castle; etc
shops: modern shopping centre; lovely antique shops; etc
transport: convenient public transport, modern metro; etc
nightlife: dance clubs; fashionable/popular restaurants; trendy cafés/theatres; etc

7 Read the rubric in Ex. 1 again. Use your answers in Ex. 6 to write your email to your English friend (80-100 words). You can use the paragraph plan in Ex. 2 to help you.

Earth Calling

Vocabulary Practice

Environmental problems

1 a. Match the environmental problems with the pictures below.

- deforestation • global warming
- reduced fish stocks • animal extinction
- air pollution • water pollution

1. smoke from factories
2. hunting wild animals
3. overfishing
4. waste from factories
5. aerosol sprays
6. excessive logging

1 ....
2 ....
3 ....
4 ....
5 ....
6 ....

b. Match the problems in Ex. 1a with the solutions (a-f). Then write sentences.

a organise tree-planting campaigns
b ban fishing in some areas
c create more national parks
d use filters on factory chimneys
e use fewer aerosol sprays
f fine factories that pollute the seas, rivers and lakes

1 d *Smoke from factories leads to air pollution. We should use filters on factory chimneys.*

2 Fill in the blanks with words from the list. There is one word you don't need to use.

- climate • scientists • rainforest • wildlife
- polluted • extinct • global

Sunday 30th November

19.00 TOXIC CROCS
A team of 1) .... tries to find out how a group of giant crocodiles survive in one of the most 2) .... rivers in Central America.

19.30 THE DODO
The dodo is one of the best known 3) .... species of bird. Find out why all the pictures we have of it are wrong.

22.30 WILD MOVIES
Cameraman Martyn Farrell explores the Amazon 4) .... and films some of its fascinating 5) ....

23.00 CORAL KILLER
Discover how 6) .... change kills coral reefs.

3 a. Match the words in the columns.

A	B
cleanup	group
environmental	people
recycling	animals
stray	park
homeless	campaign
wildlife	centre

b. Now use the phrases in Ex. 3a to complete the sentences 1-6.

1 We are taking these old newspapers to the .... in town.
2 Would you like to take part in our school's ....?
3 Poisoning .... is against the law.
4 The government has organised a housing programme to help ....
5 The Paradise .... is home to a lot of species under extinction.
6 Jane Goodall formed a young people's .... in 1991.

20

Wildlife

4 a. Put the letters into the correct order to find the names of animals.

1 kanse ....
2 nkedoy ....
3 gerit ....
4 ckoceap ....
5 rtropa ....
6 ffigare ....
7 nagutaron ....
8 ilecrodoc ....
9 uargaj ....
10 ehn ....
11 ered ....
12 kenymo ....

b. Write three animals from above for each group below, according to what they eat.

Carnivores

....
....
....

Herbivores

....
....
....

c. Answer the questions.

- Which of the animals in Ex. 4a are mammals?
- What do a snake and a crocodile have in common?
- What do a parrot and a peacock have in common?

Idioms

5 a. Fill in the gaps with words from the list.

- fish • dogs • rat • bee • bird • crocodile
- cats

1 I'm a busy .... on Tuesdays. I work in the morning and I have English classes in the afternoon.
2 The children are unusually quiet today. I smell a .... !
3 We can't leave now! It's raining .... and ....
4 Today was his first day in his new job and he felt like a .... out of water.
5 Sheila is an early .... She wakes up at 6 every morning!
6 He said he was deeply upset about the oil spill his company caused, but I don't think he really cares – he was just crying .... tears.

b. Choose three idioms and write sentences about yourself and the members of your family using them.

Verbs with prepositions

6 a. Choose the correct preposition.

Help the environment

- Take used aluminium cans **1) to/at** the recycling centre.
- Don't throw away your old magazines. Share them **2) to/with** friends.
- Prevent your local beach **3) from/of** becoming a dump. Don't drop litter.
- Join the WWF and save wild animals **4) of/from** extinction.
- Think **5) for/of** the air you breathe and try to use your car less!

... and don't forget

The earth doesn't belong **6) with/to** *us. We've just borrowed it* **7) from/of** *our children.*

b. Add three more tips to the poster on how we can help the environment.

Word formation: over-/under-

7 a. Study the table. Then, combine the words 1-3 with *over-* and *under-* to form new words.

> We add *over-* to beginning of words to express the idea of 'more than normal/usual'.
> *Bill often stays in the office till late in the evening. He works* **overtime**.
> We add *under-* to the beginning of words to express the idea of 'less than normal/usual'. *You can't vote! You are underage!*

1 paid   .... ≠ ....
2 weight .... ≠ ....
3 used   .... ≠ ....

b. Choose two adjectives and write sentences.

21

3

Grammar in Use

Exploring Grammar: Present Perfect Simple – Present Perfect Continuous

Dear Tim,
I was glad to hear that you **have just finished** your course. This is the perfect opportunity for you to come and visit me. Let me tell you about what I have been doing.
I have settled down pretty well here in Australia. I have been working for the Koala Project in Queensland since last month and I have already learned so many things about these lovely creatures. Can you believe that their population has dropped by 90% in less than a decade? This is because people have destroyed their natural habitat by cutting down the trees to build houses and roads. The staff of the Koala Project have been trying to save the koalas and their habitat for more than 15 years now, and helping them is a wonderful experience!
I have to sign off now! Write back soon and let me know if you can visit.
Love,
Katherine
P.S. In the picture, you can see my favourite koala! Isn't it cute?

1 Read the letter above and answer the questions.

  a Which tense is used in the phrase in bold? How do we form this tense? Underline all the verbs in this tense in the letter.
  b Which tense is used in the highlighted phrase? How do we form this tense?
  c What is the difference between these two tenses?
  d What are the time expressions used with the present perfect tenses? Find two examples in the letter above.

2 Fill in the gaps with the *present perfect* or the *present perfect continuous* form of the verbs in brackets.

  A: How long 1) .... (live) here, in Dublin?
  B: For six months.
  A: 2) .... (you/ever live) abroad before?
  B: No, I 3) .... (never/live) away from home before.
  A: 4) .... (you/make) friends here?
  B: Yes, quite a few.
  A: Your English is very good!
  B: Yes, I 5) .... (study) English since I was 8.
  A: Are you working anywhere?
  B: Yes, I 6) .... (work) in the local library since July.
  A: 7) .... (you/visit) the local museums yet?
  B: Yes, I 8) .... (already/be) to the History Museum.

3 Expand the questions using the correct verb forms, then write true answers about yourself.

  a you / ever / drive / a car?
  ....
  b How long / you / study / English?
  ....
  c What's/the worst film / you / ever / see?
  ....
  d How many years / you / live / here?
  ....
  e What's / the best place / you / ever / visit?
  ....

4 Look at the prompts and make sentences.

  type letters ✓
  send emails ✗
  go to the bank ✓
  go to the post office ✗
  print out documents ✓
  file documents ✗

Today is a very hectic day for John. *He has already typed some letters but he hasn't sent any emails yet.* He ....
....
....
....

have been/have gone

5 Study the examples. Then, choose the correct word in sentences 1-4.

Monday

Where's Tom?

He's gone to Paris. He's coming back tomorrow.

I've been to Paris. It's such a nice place.

Tuesday

1 Teresa has **been/gone** to the shops, but she will be back soon.
2 I have never **gone/been** to Africa!
3 "Where have you **been/gone** all day?" "I have **gone/been** at the university."
4 I'm afraid Mr Smith is not here. He's **been/gone** to the bank.

Error correction

6 Correct the mistakes in the sentences.

1 I am looking for a job for the last two weeks.
2 Nobody has seen Laura for last Sunday.
3 I haven't finished my article already.
4 He has ever tried joining an environmental group.
5 We have been members of Greenpeace since three years.
6 Have you ever saw a zebra?

Clauses of purpose

7 a. Fill in the blanks with: *in order to, for* and *so that*.

1 She took her books with her .... she could study in the library.
2 Sue phoned Ann .... invite her to a dinner party.
3 John phoned his professor .... advice.

b. Rewrite the following sentences. Use the linkers in the brackets.

Animal Planet
Monthly Report

1 We have taken the injured iguana to the vet. He must have a check up. (for)
....
2 We have visited local schools. We talked to students about wildlife. (in order to)
....
3 We have built a marine park. Seals can breed there safely. (so that)
....

Phrasal verbs: run

8 Choose the correct particle.

1 Actors always run **over/through** their lines before they go on stage.
2 I'll have to get a new passport soon. This one has run **out/out of**.
3 The robber tried to run **out of/away from** the policemen.
4 They ran **into/over** serious problems with some animals at the zoo.

Sentence transformations

9 Complete the second sentence so that it means the same as the first. Use no more than three words.

1 We have never seen such a clean zoo.
   This is the cleanest zoo we .... seen.
2 When did you last go to the zoo?
   How long .... you last went to the zoo?
3 It's two days since they fed the animals at the zoo.
   They .... the animals at the zoo for two days.
4 That was our third visit to the zoo.
   We .... the zoo three times so far.
5 The zookeeper took the monkey to the vet for a vaccination.
   The zookeeper took the monkey to the vet .... could have a vaccination.

3 Reading

1 a. How do environmental posters try to persuade us to support the environment?

b. Match the sentences in A to the meanings in B.

A
1 Don't leave the tap running for no reason.
2 The River Danube, the lifeline of Europe, is at risk of becoming polluted.
3 Take your old newspapers to the recycling centre.

B
1 Forbidding a form of action.
2 Urging a form of action.
3 Giving information about environmental problems.

2 Read the instructions for reading short texts. Number the boxes so that the instructions follow a logical order.

☐ Read options A, B and C and compare each one to the text before choosing an answer.
☐ Then, read the text carefully and think about the general meaning and its purpose.
☐ Finally, re-read the text and the answer you chose to check whether it is correct.
☐ To begin with, look at the picture for clues about where you might find the text.

3 a. Read texts 1-5 and circle the answers (*A*, *B* or *C*) that best describe them. Use the reading techniques above to help you.

1
A Do not feed the animals by hand.
B Hold your hand in this **position** to feed the animals.
C Do not touch the cage while animals are eating.

2
A Every penny you give us makes a difference.
B Please put pennies only in this box.
C If you **save** all your pennies, one day you'll be rich.

3 SIGN HERE TO SAVE OUR WOODS
A Woods are protected where you see this sign.
B Write your name if you want to protect the **woods**.
C Sign if you **wish** to join a wood-recycling project.

4 KEEP OUT OF DIRECT SUNLIGHT
A Don't use the **contents** on a sunny day.
B Don't use the contents on **shiny** things.
C Sunlight can damage the contents.

5 STOP! If you buy souvenirs made with bird feathers or other animal parts, you run the risk of getting arrested.
A You may be arrested if you buy souvenirs with wild animals on them.
B You may be **arrested** if you buy souvenirs made of animal parts.
C Souvenirs made of animal parts are risky for your health.

b. Answer the questions.

1 Which of the texts (1-5) suggest possible danger?
2 What might happen if you don't pay attention to notices 1, 4 and 5?
3 Which notices encourage you to help a good cause?

4 Explain the words in bold in the answers A-C in Ex. 3a. You can use your dictionary. Then, use the words in sentences of your own.

24

Listening & Speaking

Caring for the planet

1 a. Are you a friend of the Earth? Read the checklist and circle *Yes* or *No*.

b. Now write sentences, as in the example.

I've watched a few wildlife programmes recently, but I haven't tried to recycle things at home yet. I've ...

Are you a friend of the Earth?

Have you:
- watched a wildlife programme on TV recently? Yes/No
- tried to recycle everyday items at home? Yes/No
- picked up litter from a beach or the countryside? Yes/No
- helped an animal that was sick? Yes/No
- tried to avoid buying non-recyclable goods? Yes/No
- encouraged your friends/family to do the above? Yes/No

Becoming a member

2 a. Read the phrases in the box. What do you expect the dialogue to be about? Read through and check, then choose phrases from the box to complete the dialogue.

> ▶ *Could you tell me a little more about your organisation?*
> ▶ *What can I do to help?*
> ▶ *I would like to become a member of ...*
> ▶ *How much does membership cost?*
> ▶ *Can I have your name and address ...?*

A: Excuse me. Would you like to make a small donation to MOm?
B: Well, maybe but, em ... 1) .... ?
A: Certainly! MOm is an environmental organisation that studies and protects the Mediterranean Monk Seal, which is in danger of becoming extinct.
B: Really? I had no idea. Is that because of pollution?
A: Actually, it's mainly due to overfishing. Many seals get caught in fishing nets.
B: How awful! So 2) .... ?
A: How about becoming a member of MOm?
B: I'd love to, but I'm a student and I don't think I can afford it. By the way, 3) .... ?
A: Well, there are different types of membership, but, as a student, you can become a member for just £20 a year. Then you will receive an information pack about MOm's activities, your membership card and regular newsletters.
B: £20? That seems reasonable. I'll do that, then!
A: Super! 4) ...., please?
B: It's Ann Sullivan and I live at 7, Oxford Road, Manchester, M10 9PL ...

b. Find and underline phrases or words in the dialogue that mean:

1 to give to a charity or an organisation
2 'I can't pay for it'
3 to no longer exist
4 'I didn't know about it'
5 not too high (for prices)

c. You are thinking of becoming a member of an environmental organisation called 'GREEN PLANET'. What questions would you ask about it?

Public speaking

3 🎧 You will hear someone giving advice about speeches and presentations. Try to guess what the missing words are. Listen and check.

Successful Speeches & Presentations
Prepare
You won't feel 1) .... if you know what to say.
Using notes
Keep notes 2) ...., clear and easy to read.
Equipment
Check the equipment 3) .... you begin speaking.
Speaking
Speak 4) .... than you think you need to.
Forgotten what to say?
Staying 5) .... will help you remember.
Be professional
Successful speakers are 6) .... and enthusiastic.

3

Writing (a letter giving news)

Getting started

1 Read the rubric and underline the key words. What should you include in your letter?

- You have taken part in a special 'Clean up our town' campaign. Write a letter to your English pen-friend telling him/her all about it. In your letter you should:
  - say when, where and why the event took place.
  - describe what people did and how you helped.

Let's look closer

2 a. Read the letter and put the topic sentences (1-3) in the right paragraphs. There is one extra sentence you do not need to use.

1 We worked in small groups.
2 In the beginning, I didn't know which group to join.
3 Last week there was a cleanup campaign in my town.

Hi Mike,

How are you? I've heard you joined Greenpeace! That's great! Actually, I've also done something to help the environment.

a) ....

The Scout group, my school and the sports club organised a campaign. We wanted to clean up our town's streets and parks because they were full of litter after the annual Flower Festival.

b) ....

Each group had its own team leader. The first group picked up litter off the streets and put it into plastic bags. Then, the second group took the bags to the recycling centre outside town. The third group cleaned up the two big parks in the city centre. I was responsible for sorting the rubbish into different bags for the recycling process. It was pretty hard work, but very rewarding!

You should come and visit our town now that it's nice and clean! I hope to see you soon.

Love,
Mark

Introduction
(Para 1) *Opening remarks, reason for writing*

(Para 2) ....
....
....

(Para 3) ....
....
....

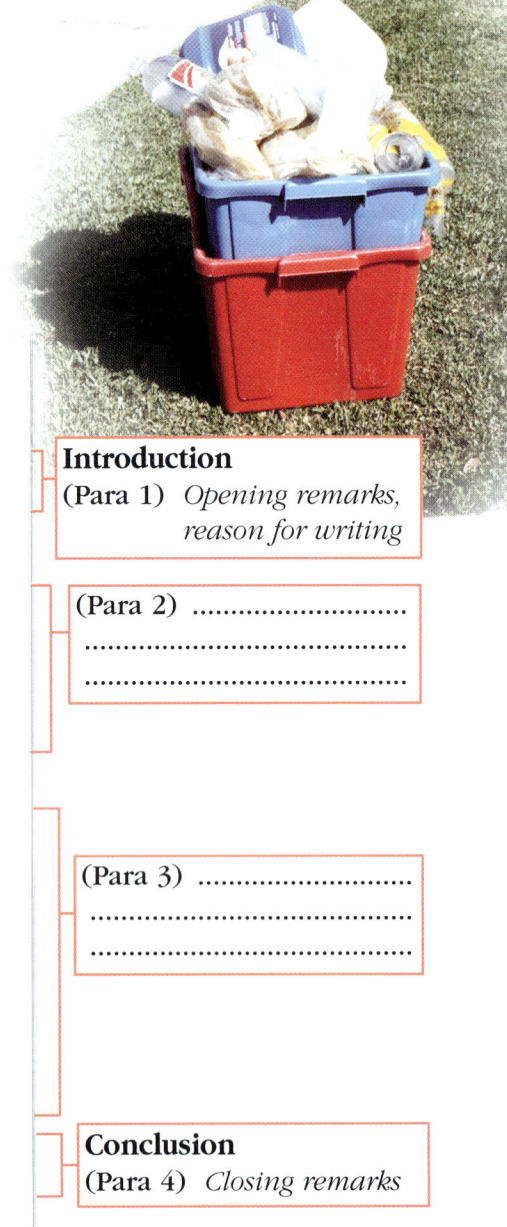

Conclusion
(Para 4) *Closing remarks*

b. Complete the letter plan.

26

Opening/Closing remarks

3 a. Which of the expressions below are opening remarks and which are closing remarks? Mark the sentences *(O)* for opening or *(C)* for closing.

Write soon.	.....
See you soon.	.....
I thought you might be interested to hear about/know that …	.....
Do drop me a line.	.....
I look forward to hearing from you.	.....
This is just to let you know that …	.....

b. Choose expressions from the box to give Mike's letter a different beginning and a different ending.

Linkers

4 a. Read the letter in Ex. 2 again and find:

- a word that links similar ideas.
- a word stating the reason for something.
- a word that shows sequence

b. Now use these linkers to join the sentences below.

1 The beach was dirty. The tourists had left their rubbish behind.
....
....

2 First, we chose a group leader. We came up with an action plan.
....
....

3 We picked the plastic bags out of the water. We picked up all the tin cans on the beach.
....

Your turn

5 a. Read the rubric and underline the key words/phrases.

> You are taking part in a conservation project to save the sea turtle in a foreign country this summer. Write a letter to your English pen-friend, telling him/her all about it. In your letter you should:
>
> - explain what the project is about
> - say what your duties are
> - invite your friend to visit you

b. Which of the following sentences can be used as topic sentences?

a I've joined a project to save the sea turtle.
b For example, some people hunt sea turtles and steal their eggs.
c We work in small groups doing a variety of tasks.
d I'm having a wonderful time here in Costa Rica.

Supporting sentences

Supporting sentences expand on topic sentences (i.e. sentences which summarise the paragraph) and give more information.
Topic sentence:
The clean-up campaign was a great success.
Supporting sentences:
We managed to pick up all the litter in the town centre and paint over all the graffiti. We've also...

6 In pairs, use the prompts to write supporting sentences for the topic sentences in Ex. 5.

- sea turtles • endangered species
- need our protection • make sure turtles breed
- babies survive

- watch turtles • protect them • hunters
- patrol beach • make sure turtles safe
- gather eggs • nests • take them to special hatchery • release baby turtles into ocean

- stay with local family • experience life in tiny seaside village • eat local dishes • learn customs and traditions

7 Use your answers in Exs 5 & 6 to write your letter to your friend (120-180 words). You can use the plan in Ex. 2 to help you.

27

Travellers' Tales

Amsterdam

The Seychelles

Salzburg

Helsinki

Egypt

Vocabulary Practice

Types of holidays

1 Put the words in the right column, then make sentences, as in the example.

- stylish shops and cafés
- white sand and crystal clear waters
- a skiing holiday
- sightseeing holiday
- a beach holiday
- snow-capped mountain peaks
- beautiful countryside
- a camping holiday
- a city break
- ancient monuments

Egypt, with its ancient monuments, is ideal for a sightseeing holiday.

Destination	Attractions	Type of holiday
Egypt	ancient monuments	sightseeing holiday
Amsterdam		
Helsinki		
Salzburg		
The Seychelles		

2 Imagine you are going on a trip to the Seychelles. Which 5 of these objects would you take and why? Complete the list.

A hiking boots
B backpack
C passport
D sunscreen
E beach ball
F beach towel
G beach umbrella

1 sunscreen – for sun protection
2 backpack – easier to carry around
3 ....
4 ....
5 ....

Weather

3 Find 12 words related to weather. Use them to describe the weather in your country today.

S	U	N	N	Y	O	C	O	L	D
E	S	W	E	T	R	C	O	O	W
C	N	A	J	M	D	R	Y	T	I
E	O	R	A	I	N	Y	J	M	N
R	W	M	S	L	C	O	O	L	D
E	Y	F	D	D	F	O	G	G	Y
Q	W	P	L	E	A	S	A	N	T

Across: ....
....
Down: ....
....

Today, ...

Expressing feelings

4 a. Match the words to the pictures. Then, write sentences.

• angry/computer crashed • fed up/no one to play with • pleased/got job • nervous/about interview • frightened/by the sight of blood

1 *She was fed up because she had no one to play with.*

b. Underline the correct word.

1 I can't believe you liked the concert! It was so **bored/boring**.
2 The service in the hotel was very **disappointed/ disappointing**.
3 My boss is quite **satisfied/satisfying** with my work.
4 Ann is not **interested/interesting** in sports at all.
5 'The Lord of the Rings' is a **fascinated/ fascinating** film.

Means of transport

5 Use *on* or *by* and a means of transport to complete the following sentences.

1 My dad travels to work .... He enjoys driving a lot.
2 He goes to school .... He likes riding through the quiet streets.
3 To get to the island you have to travel ....
4 I go to work .... It's just a ten-minute walk.
5 Business people fly very often because travelling .... is faster.

Words often confused

6 a. Fill in: *trip*, *voyage*, *journey*.

1 I'm going on a two-day business .... to Brussels next week.
2 In 1492, Christopher Columbus went on his first .... across the Atlantic Ocean.
3 The .... from Brighton to London takes about 1½ hrs by train.

b. Fill in: *expedition*, *cruise*, *trek*.

1 Last summer, we went on a(n) .... around the Mediterranean.
2 In May 2003, 24 scientists went on a(n) .... to find the lost city of Atlantis.
3 Last May we went on a(n) .... through the jungle. It was amazing.

Word formation: Forming opposites

il-, *im-*, *in-*, and *ir-* are added to the beginning of words to form words with the opposite meaning. *il-* is added to words beginning with **l**, *ir-* is added to words beginning with **r** and *im-* is added to the words beginning with **m**, **b** or **p**.

7 Use the prefixes *il-*, *im-*, *in-* or *ir-* to form the opposites of the following adjectives. Then, use them to complete the sentences (1-5).

patient	legal ....
possible	secure ....
responsible	complete ....
logical	rational ....
mature	discreet ....

1 I'm sorry, but I can't meet you at 8:00. It's ....
2 It was very .... of you to leave your sister to come home by herself.
3 After losing her job, Diana started feeling very ....
4 It's .... to buy souvenirs made from endangered species.
5 This list is .... There are some names missing.

29

4

Grammar in Use

Exploring Grammar:
Past simple/continuous

1 Read the text and answer questions 1-6.

Aesop's Fables
The Lion and the Mouse

One day, while a lion was sleeping, a mouse ran over his face and woke him up. The lion got angry, caught the mouse and threatened to kill him. *While he was holding the mouse tight, it was crying for help.* It said: "If you spare my life, I will repay your kindness." The lion laughed and set it free. Weeks later, some hunters caught the lion and tied him up. As the lion was roaring for help, the mouse appeared, cut the ropes with his teeth and said: "Now you know that even a mouse can do a lion a big favour."

1 Read the first sentence. What action was in progress when something else happened? What tense is the action in?
2 What happened after that? What tense are the actions in?
3 Which word can replace *while* in the beginning of the fable without changing the meaning?
4 How many actions take place in the sentence in italics? What is the time relationship between them?
5 Can you find another example of an interrupted action in the fable?
6 Can you find examples of past actions which happened one after the other?

2 Read the extract and fill in the blanks using the *past simple* or the *past continuous* of the verbs in brackets.

Last Saturday, my sister and I 1) .... (catch) the 9 o'clock train to Glasgow. We got as far as Dumfries when the train 2) .... (break) down. While we 3) .... (wait) for the mechanics to arrive and fix the train, we 4) .... (decide) to take a walk through the countryside. The area was so picturesque that, instead of going on to Glasgow, we 5) .... (spend) the rest of our weekend there!

3 Complete the sentences in your own words.

1 He was talking on the phone when ....
2 While I was sitting an exam, the ....
3 She was waiting for a bus when, all of a sudden, ...
4 It was a cold winter's day. The wind was blowing and ....
5 They were surfing the net when ....

4 Write a short paragraph using the *past simple* and *past continuous* about an unusual journey you had. Use the text in Ex. 2 as a model.

Used to/would

5 a. Fill: *used to* or *would*. In which sentences can you use both?

1 My grandfather .... sleep after lunch every afternoon.
2 He .... take karate lessons when he was 15 years old.
3 When I was young, I .... play the guitar every day.
4 Tony .... have a boat when he was 15.
5 When Jim was a child, his favourite food .... be pasta.

b. Use the prompts below to write sentences about the habits you had when you were seven.

- summer holidays • after school
- at night • at the weekends
- on Sunday mornings

When I was seven, I used to spend my summer holidays in my father's hometown.

Linkers

6 Join the following sentences, using *but*, *because*, *when*, *then* and *as*.

1 He felt anxious. He couldn't find his hand luggage.
....
2 Fiona had booked a room. The receptionist couldn't find the booking.
....
3 I took my bags and locked the doors. I waited outside for the taxi to come.
....
4 He was about to pay his hotel bill. He realised his wallet wasn't in his bag.
....
5 Graham was listening to his favourite CD. He was driving back home.
....

Phrasal verbs: come

7 Choose the correct particle.

1 I took lots of photographs of Berlin, but only a few came **round/out**.
2 Sandra comes **across/up** as being a very kind girl, doesn't she?
3 I didn't agree with Trevor at first, but I came **across/round** to his way of thinking in the end.
4 Shane is clever. He often comes **up/out** with excellent suggestions.

Article (a/an/the/–)

8 Look at the encyclopedia entry about Alaska and fill in *a, an* or *the* when necessary.

Alaska

Alaska is **1)** .... largest state in **2)** .... USA, with **3)** .... population of 634,892. **4)** .... name Alaska comes from **5)** .... old word, 'Alyeska', meaning 'great land'. Alaska officially became **6)** .... 49th state in 1959. Before 1959, Alaska was **7)** .... territory and not **8)** .... state. **9)** .... capital of **10)** .... Alaska is **11)** .... Juneau, located in **12)** .... southeast region. Juneau has **13)** .... population of 30,684. In Barrow, Alaska's northernmost village far above the Arctic Circle, **14)** .... sun doesn't set for 84 days!

Sentence transformations

9 Complete the second sentence so that it means the same as the first. Use no more than three words.

1 While I was tidying my desk, I found an old travel guide.
   While I was tidying my desk, I came .... travel guide.
2 There were travelling along the coast when their car broke down.
   Their car broke down .... travelling along the coast.
3 As a student, she travelled abroad every year.
   When she was a student, she .... travel abroad every year.
4 Tony got stuck in traffic so he missed his flight.
   Tony missed his flight .... he got stuck in traffic.
5 Sheila had a car accident on her way to the station.
   While Sheila .... the station, she had an accident.

4

Reading

1 a. Look at the layout of the text. Do you think it is:

1 a bus itinerary?
2 a festival programme?
3 a package holiday brochure?

b. Read the title, and the first sentence of the introduction. What kind of holiday do you think is being advertised?

1 a honeymoon deal
2 a cruise
3 an adventure holiday

2 a. Read through the text and check your answers in Ex. 1.

b. Read the text and mark the statements below true *(T)* or false *(F)*.

1 The whole holiday lasts 15 days. .....
2 You have to pay for some of your meals. .....
3 Quito is the capital of Ecuador. .....
4 The passage mentions two different ways of seeing the Amazon rainforest. .....
5 During the Amazon excursion you may see some rare plants and animals. .....
6 There are places of cultural interest to see in Quito. .....
7 You have to wear warm clothes to go to the Galapagos Islands. .....
8 The trip to the Galapagos Islands includes a chance to see some marine life. .....
9 You have some time on your own before dinner on the yacht. .....
10 On the eighth night, you leave for the islands by plane. .....

3 Use your dictionary to find the meanings of the words in bold. Then, write sentences using them.

4 Would you enjoy a holiday like the one described in the text? Why (not)?

Galapagos with Amazon Jungle and Quito Ecuador

Join us on this thrilling **fortnight** of adventure in the tropics and explore a world that time has forgotten. You will see the Amazon rainforest, as well as the Galapagos Islands and historic Quito. All travel **expenses**, excursions and most meals are included in the price.

Itinerary

Day 1: Arrival in Quito, Ecuador. Stay **overnight** in the capital city of Ecuador at a luxury hotel.

Days 2-6: We depart early and **head** downriver by canoe into the jungle. Here we spend five days exploring the Amazon jungle on foot, by canoe and from a platform built 130ft above the rainforest floor in a giant kapok tree. We will have the chance to see hundreds of species of exotic and rare flowers, and we might also see endangered mammals such as jaguars and the pink river dolphin.
When it's time to **depart**, we **motor** back **upriver** for a flight to Quito and an overnight stay at the Hilton Colon Quito. Dinner is on you tonight.

Day 7: Quito. We spend the day sightseeing in the oldest city in South America. It is also a centre of learning, and its university **dates from** 1586. You will have the opportunity to explore Quito's peaceful squares and many museums, including the Museum of Anthropology and the Municipal Museum of Art.

Day 8: Fly to the Galapagos Islands. Make sure to dress for the warm weather! There we meet our **guide** and head for the Santa Cruz mountains by coach. We will see many plant species, visit two **lava sink holes**, and enjoy lunch at a cosy country restaurant. After lunch we **search for** giant tortoises. Then we're off to the Hotel Galapagos to **unwind** and say hello to marine iguanas. In the afternoon, we tour Academy Bay by boat and have a little time to **hang out** before boarding our yacht for dinner.

Days 9-14: During the night we **weigh anchor** and **set off** for the first of our island stops. For the next six days we cruise around the islands.

Day 15: We fly back to Quito and depart for home or go on other adventures!

4

Listening & Speaking
Travel information

1 a. Read the first exchange in the dialogue. Who is the man (B) talking to? Why do you think he has called? Read and check.

A: Good morning, sir. Can I help you?
B: 1) ………………………… flights to Vienna.
A: When would you like to travel?
B: Thursday morning. I'm flying one way.
A: 2) ………………………… . There's a flight at 08:15 and another at 11:45.
B: Sorry, did you say 08:15?
A: 3) ………………………… .
B: 4) ………………………… how long the flight is?
A: Yes ... it takes 2 hours and 10 minutes.
B: And 5) ………………………… , please?
A: It's €140.
B: All right, then. 6) ………………………… the 11:45 flight.

b. Use expressions from the box to complete the gaps (1-6) in the dialogue.

Asking for information/services	Confirming
I'd like some information about ... I'd like a ticket for ... I'd like to book a room for (5th and 6th July). Could you tell me ...? How much is it ...	Just a moment, I'll check. Right, I've got that. Yes, that's right. Sorry, that's not correct.

c. In pairs, act out a similar dialogue. Use the expressions in the box in Ex. 1b.

Hotel facilities / service

2 Which are the most important facilities to you? Why? Write sentences, as in the example.

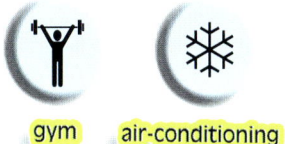

restaurant, swimming pool, hairdresser's, television, car park, gym, air-conditioning, laundry, sauna, room

The car park is important to me because I need to keep my car safe.

Complaining

3 Choose the correct response: *a* or *b*.

1 A: I'd like to complain about the room service. It's so slow.
   B: a I'm afraid there's no record of that booking, sir.
      b I do apologise, sir.

2 A: What do you think of the children's playground?
   B: a I think it is open all day.
      b It's fine.

3 A: How do you find the laundry service?
   B: a It's very good indeed.
      b It's at the end of the hall, sir.

4 A: I'm sorry, madam, but breakfast is only served between 8:30am and 9am.
   B: a That's outrageous!
      b I'm so terribly sorry.

5 A: Excuse me. There are no towels in our room.
   B: a Oh! That's terrible, isn't it?
      b I'm sorry. I'll send some up immediately.

Holiday Complaints

4 a. What complaints could someone have while on holiday in a seaside hotel?

b. You will hear a conversation about someone's holiday. Decide if each sentence is correct or incorrect. If it is correct, tick **Yes**. If not, tick **No**.

		Yes	No
1	There was no restaurant at the hotel Tracey stayed at.	☐	☐
2	Dave is surprised by what Tracey says about the room service.	☐	☐
3	Tracey spent a lot of time at the beach.	☐	☐
4	Tracey and her family watched a lot of TV while on holiday.	☐	☐
5	Tracey's hotel room wasn't very clean.	☐	☐
6	Tracey will not go to the same place next year.	☐	☐

c. What was your last holiday like? Were there any problems?

4

Writing (a story)

Getting started

1 Read the rubric. What could the most important event be? Who can the main character(s) be?

- Your English teacher has asked you to write a short story entitled *A Holiday to Remember*. The best stories will be published in the school magazine.

Let's look closer

2 The paragraphs in the story have been mixed up. Put them in the right order. Which paragraph contains the most dramatic event (climax event)?

A holiday to remember

A One night I was driving along the road when I noticed that there were no more signposts. Suddenly, I realised that we were lost. There were no lights anywhere, so I stopped the camper van for the night.

B After a while, a boat arrived and pulled us back to the beach. A couple of hours later we were home, safe and sound! From then on, we decided to stay in a hotel for our holidays.

C I was sick and tired of going to the same place every year, so last year my family and I decided to travel around Brittany for two weeks in a camper van.

D The following day, I woke up and the camper van was moving by itself. We were floating on the sea! I called for help immediately. Meanwhile, my wife was trying to stop water from coming into the camper van.

Sequence of events

3 List the events in the story in chronological order. Which words/expressions helped you to put the events in the right order?

4 Complete the sentences using the verbs in brackets in the past simple or past continuous.

1 It .... (rain) heavily as we .... (leave) the house that morning.
2 She .... (look) around and saw that the boat .... (sail) away.
3 He .... (need) a holiday, so he .... (decide) to book a week in Spain.
4 I quickly .... (call) the fire brigade. Meanwhile, Pete .... (throw) water on the flames.
5 When we .... (arrive) at the hotel, we .... (realise) our luggage was missing.
6 Suddenly, they .... (see) a light in the distance and they knew someone .... (come) to rescue them.
7 She .... (sunbathe) on the beach when she .... (hear) a strange noise.
8 When he .... (open) his eyes, he thought that he .... (dream).

Joining sentences

5 Complete the sentences using *and*, *so* or *but*.

1 It was pouring with rain, ... we decided to stay in the hotel.
2 We wanted to go on holiday, ... we didn't have enough money.
3 They put their suitcases in the car .... set off for the airport.
4 Jane tried to lift the box, ... it was far too heavy.
5 The most beautiful spot on the campsite was empty, ... we decided to put up our tent there.
6 It was late at night .... the stars were shining in the black sky.

Time Linkers

6 Rewrite the following sentences using appropriate linking words.

> First, After that, Then/Next, Immediately, While, The following day, As soon as, In the end, Meanwhile, Finally, Suddenly, After a while

1. I called the police. Dave tried to catch the thief.
   I called the police. Meanwhile, David tried to catch the thief.
   While I called the police, David tried to catch the thief.
2. We were walking along the beach. We heard somebody shouting.
3. She saw the flames. She called the fire brigade.
4. They called for help. A man came and rescued them.
5. Kate looked everywhere for her keys. She found them under her bed.
6. We checked into the hotel. We went to our room and unpacked.
7. He fell fast asleep. He woke up early and drove out to the lake.
8. The children played in the sea. Their parents relaxed on the beach.

Beginnings/Endings

> **To start a story** you need to think of:
> – the main character(s)
> – time of year/weather
> – place the story takes place
> – what the main characters were doing

7 Look at the picture and the prompts and write the beginning of a story entitled *"A Day to Remember"*. Include all the points mentioned above.

[last Friday afternoon] [Tony] [Kitchen]

> **To end a story** you need to think of:
> – what happened in the end
> – how the character(s) felt

8 Now, look at the picture and write an ending. Write what happened in the end and how the main character felt.

[restaurant] [happy] [Tony & his dad]

Your turn

9 Read the rubric, underline the key words, then answer the questions in the plan.

> Your English teacher has asked you to write a short story entitled *A Day to Remember*.

Plan

Drafting your story
Introduction
(Para 1)   Who was/were the main character(s)?
           here were they?
           When did the story take place?
           What were they doing?

Main Body
(Paras 2-3)   What happened? List the events in the order they happened and the climax event.

Conclusion
(Para 4)   What happened in the end?
           How did the characters feel?

10 Now write your story (80-100 words).

On Offer

Vocabulary Practice

Shops & Shopping

1 Fill in the gaps with the names of the shops.

Things to do...

- Take my suit to the d.......... -c..........
- Buy some fish from the f..............
- Get Jenny some cakes from the b.............. and buy the kids some chocolates at the c..............
- Visit the s.............. for envelopes and pens.
- Drop by the c.............. for a packet of aspirins.

2 a. Read the advertisements and find words related to the categories below. Add two more words to each category.

Classified Ads

For sale – beautiful, full-length plain white silk wedding dress. Good as new. Only worn once. £1,000. Tel: 0201 58 6933

Bargain! Antique blue and white china tea set with a floral design plus three large square wooden serving trays. £300. 6973444888

Wanted to buy – a blue and green checked tartan kilt to fit a ten-year-old boy. Call **Mr Brown** on 0772568741

For sale – small round glass coffee table. £50. Tel: 0254 587963

Material: ....
Shape: ....
Colour: ....
Pattern: ....

b. Use words from Ex. 2a to describe the objects below, as in the example.

It's a rectangular plain brown leather briefcase.

briefcase

shorts — hat — basketball — wallet

Clothes

3 a. Label the items shown in the pictures. Then, describe what the people are wearing, as in the example.

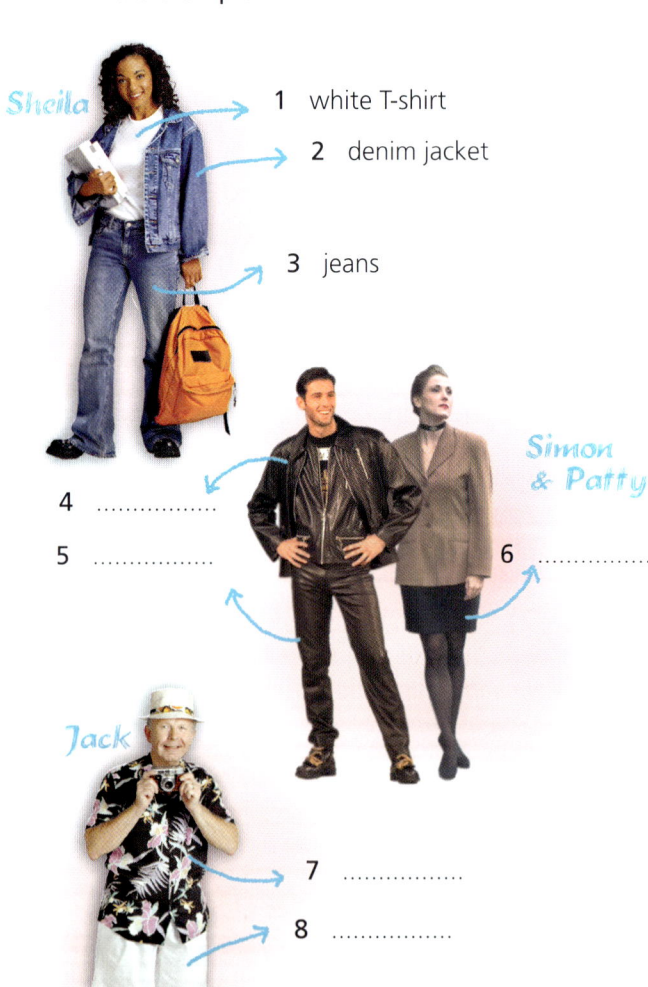

Sheila
1 white T-shirt
2 denim jacket
3 jeans

Simon & Patty
4 ....
5 ....
6 ....

Jack
7 ....
8 ....
9 socks
10 ....

Sheila is wearing a denim jacket, a white T-shirt, a pair of blue jeans and a pair of boots.

36

b. Take a look in your wardrobe and complete the sentences.

1. My favourite trousers *are my plain cotton white ones*.
2. My favourite T-shirt is ....
3. My favourite shoes are ....
4. I hate wearing ....
5. I can't stand ....

Prices

4 Look at the items on sale and their prices and write the amounts in full.

£20 — pocket calculator
£1.20 — ice cream
£29.99 — shoes

1. A pocket calculator costs ....
2. ....
3. ....

Opposites

5 Complete the following exchanges with the opposites of the words in bold.

1. A: Is this bag too **plain**?
   B: Yes. Why don't you get a f................ one?
2. A: I simply can't afford to buy a b................ n................ car.
   B: Well, what about a **second-hand** one?
3. A: Have you **saved** any money for your holiday, yet?
   B: Not really. I've s................ all my salary on new clothes.
4. A: Ann always wears **old-fashioned** clothes.
   B: Really? Her twin sister is very t................ .
5. A: Do you wear c................ clothes at work?
   B: No, we have to be dressed in **formal** clothes.

Words with prepositions

If you do something **online**, you do it using the Internet.
When somone is **in line**, for something they are likely to get it.
If something is **on the line**, you may lose it or harm it as a result of what you do or the situation you are in.
If someone steps **out of line**, they disobey someone or behave in an unacceptable way.

6 Fill in the blanks with the correct phrase.

1. The soldier was punished because he stepped ....
2. I found this great website and I bought a couple of books ....
3. Ian has worked really hard ths year he must be .... for a promotion.
4. He put everything .... when he started his own business.

Word formation: Forming verbs from adjectives

7 Form verbs from the adjectives and then put them in the blanks.

We add **-en** or **-n** to a noun or adjective to make a verb meaning 'to make more of something'.

length *lengthen*   tight ....
short ....   sharp ....
wide ....   loose ....

1. These trousers are too long. Can you .... them for me, please?
2. It's a narrow road, but it .... in some places so that cars can pass each other.
3. My tie is too tight. Can you .... it, please?
4. I can't cut anything with this knife. I must .... its blade.
5. The screws on this cupboard door are loose. You should .... them.

37

5

Grammar in Use

Exploring Grammar: Modals

Let's go Johnny, we have to buy lots of things for the party tonight.

We must be back before 4 pm remember.

Yes you can, but you mustn't make a mess of the shelves.

OK then.

OK, but you don't have to go so fast, Dad.

Oh yes! Can I get some chocolate biscuits?

Look! These have got chocolate chips! They must be delicious. Can I get them Dad?

Oh great! I can't wait for the party.

1 Read the dialogue and answer the following questions.

1. Which verbs express obligation? What's the difference between them?
2. Which verb expresses absence of necessity?
3. Who's asking for permission? Underline the appropriate sentence. How do we ask for permission in formal situations?
4. Which phrase in the dialogue expresses prohibition?
5. Who's making an assumption? Underline the sentence. Then turn it into its negative form. Do you notice any changes?

2 a. You are the owner of a café. You have just hired a new waitress and you are talking to her about her duties and obligations. Fill in the gaps with *must/ mustn't/have to/don't have to*.

A: You start work at 8:45 every afternoon, Sonia. Don't forget that we open at nine, so you 1) .... be late.
B: Do I 2) .... wear a uniform?
A: No, but you 3) .... wear comfortable shoes. Being a waitress means that you 4) .... spend a lot of time on your feet.
B: Right.
A: Now, you 5) .... take the customers' orders as soon as they arrive. Remember, you 6) .... keep them waiting! And you 7) .... always be polite to the customers.
B: Yes, of course. What about the washing-up?
A: You 8) .... wash up. Linda does that.

b. In pairs, continue the dialogue.

Modals: Past Forms

3 Interview your parents and complete the following sentences.

When he was 6, my father could ...
When she was four, my mother couldn't ...
When he was a student, my father had to ...

Now write sentences about yourself, using *could, wasn't able to* and *had to*. Use the prompts below.

toddler   7 years old

38

Making assumptions

4 Look at the pictures and make assumptions. You can use the prompts as well as your own ideas.

1 (rich/poor)
He must be rich.
He can't be poor.
He may be a businessman.

(cold/hot)
....
....
....

2

3 (at work/on holiday)
....
....
....

(excited/scared)
....
....
....

4

Requests: can, could, may

5 Write questions for the following situations. Ask:

1 your boss ...
   a if you can leave work early
   ....
   b if you can use the company car
   ....

2 a shop assistant ...
   a if you can try a pair of shoes on
   ....
   b if you can have a discount
   ....

3 your best friend ...
   a if you can visit him/her later tonight
   ....
   b if you can go with him/her to the cinema
   ....

Too/enough

6 You bought your family's Christmas presents in a hurry. When they opened them, they realised something was wrong. Use *too/enough* and the adjectives in brackets to complete the following exchanges.

1 A: Do you like the dress, Mum?
   B: Well, it's lovely, but it's .... (short) for me to wear!
2 A: Dad, what about your pair of trousers?
   B: I love the colour, but I'm afraid they aren't .... (long).
3 A: Timmy, what about your computer game?
   B: It's great, but it's for under ten-year-olds and I'm 17! It's .... (challenging)!
4 A: Andy, have you tried your new tracksuit on?
   B: Yes, but it looks better on Timmy! It's .... (small) for me.
5 A: How about your new shoes, Grandma?
   B: They've got high heels! They aren't .... (comfortable) I'm afraid.

Phrasal verbs: look

7 Choose the correct particle to complete the phrasal verbs.

1 When I don't know what a word means, I look it **up/for** in a dictionary.
2 Look **out/up**! That car's coming this way.
3 Most children look **out/up to** their parents.
4 Jerry doesn't need any help. He can look **for/after** himself.

Sentence transformations

8 For each sentence, complete the second sentence so that it means the same as the first one. Use no more than three words.

1 I think he is the shop assistant, but I'm not sure.
   He .... the shop assistant.
2 I would like a glass of water.
   May .... glass of water, please?
3 This pair of jeans is not long enough for me.
   This pair of jeans is .... for me.
4 She lost her wallet so she couldn't pay for her shopping.
   She lost her wallet so she .... to pay for her shopping.
5 I can't wait to open my birthday presents!
   I am .... opening my birthday presents!

39

5 Reading

1 a. Read the title of the text. What do you expect to read? Read the text and check.

b. Underline the topic sentences in the main body paragraphs of the text. Which paragraph:

1 encourages you to ask what people want? ....
2 gives advice about buying gifts for people you know well? ....
3 tells you what to avoid? ....
4 helps you with buying gifts for people you haven't seen for a long time? ....

2 Read the text and mark statements 1-10 true *(T)* or false *(F)*.

The Perfect Gift

A If you are the person that everyone turns to when they need gift-giving advice, then don't read any further. Unfortunately, for most of us, choosing the right gift for a loved one can often be a frustrating experience. Here are some tips that should make gift shopping a lot less confusing.

B Choosing a gift for someone you spend a lot of time with is relatively easy. Simply pay attention to what they look at when you go shopping together.

C And what about those you don't see very often? Simply ask their friends or family for advice. They are the ones who know best what the person is interested in as well as what they want or need.

D Sometimes, it's much easier to just ask people what they want. Children will be happy to tell you but adults tend to be a little less direct. In that case, try to find out what other people give them and get them something related to their hobbies or interests.

E Always make sure that the presents you buy can be returned. Never buy gifts from a shop that has no refund or exchange policy. If you are buying through the Internet, find out what options you have if the product is not satisfactory.

F Personally, whenever I don't know what to get someone, I buy them a gift voucher. This way, the person in question can choose their own gift and you will have gained the reputation of being the perfect gift giver.

1 If you know how to choose presents, you don't need to read this article. ....
2 Most people find it easy to shop for presents. ....
3 Take people you know well shopping to buy them their gift. ....
4 If you don't see a person very often, buy a gift their family will like. ....
5 Children say what presents they want. ....
6 Adults don't always tell you what they want for a present. ....
7 Don't buy anything that you can't take back to the shop. ....
8 Buying gifts from the Internet should be avoided. ....
9 A gift voucher is an award given to perfect gift givers. ....
10 Most people don't like getting gift vouchers as presents. ....

3 a. Read the text again. Which two pieces of advice do you find most useful?

b. What birthday present would you buy your best friend/a distant cousin of yours? Why?

40

Listening & Speaking
Shopping for clothes

1 a. Complete the conversation between a shop assistant and a customer with the phrases A-J. There are three extra phrases you do not need to use.

A: [1] ....
B: Yes, please. I'm looking for a summer dress.
A: [2] ....
B: Well, it's beautiful but I'm after something a bit more casual.
A: [3] ....
B: That's exactly what I'm looking for. Could I try it on please?
A: [4] ....
B: 12.
A: [5] ....
B: I'm sorry but it doesn't fit me very well. Do you have it in a larger size?
A: [6] ....
B: That's it! It suits me perfectly! How much is it?
A: [7] ....
B: That's a bargain!

A Can I help you, madam?
B For what occasion?
C Then, you'll certainly like this cotton one.
D Here you are. The fitting rooms are over there on your right.
E It's very cheap, indeed.
F It's £20 down from £40.
G No, I'm afraid this is not for sale.
H What about this silk one?
I Of course. What size are you?
J Certainly, madam. Here is a size 14.

b. In pairs, act out similar dialogues.

2 a. Read sentences 1-6 in Ex. 2b. What assumptions can you make about Samantha and Bill? Think about:

- their relationship • place they are
- reason they are there

Listen and check your answers.

b. Listen and tick true (T) or false (F).

		T	F
1	Samantha's family will be at the wedding.	.....	.....
2	Bill hasn't got a black suit.	.....	.....
3	Bill doesn't like grey suits.	.....	.....
4	Samantha thinks the shoes are cheap.	.....	.....
5	The men's shop is closing.	.....	.....
6	Bill doesn't want to wear his old suit.	.....	.....

Complimenting

3 a. Complete the exchanges with sentences from the box.

- Well, it looks really nice on you.
- It smells wonderful!
- It suits you perfectly!
- It fits you really well!

1 A: Is this jacket my size?
  B: Certainly! ....
2 A: I think this blue hat matches my eyes.
  B: You're right! ....
3 A: What do you think of my new perfume?
  B: Wow! ....
4 A: Do you think I should buy this?
  B: ....

b. In pairs, act out similar dialogues.

Describing pictures

4 Describe the picture. Think about:

- where the people are.
- what they are wearing/doing.
- what they are talking about.
- what their feelings are.

41

5

Writing (a report assessing good & bad points)

Getting started

1 Read the rubric and underline the key words/phrases then answer the questions below.

• Who is going to read the report?   • How many paragraphs will your report have?

> You work for a travel magazine. Your editor has asked you to write a report assessing the suitability of a local flea market for a shopping trip. Write your report, describing the facilities, shops and prices, and give your recommendation.

Let's look closer

2 a. Read the report and underline the correct words in bold.

To: Timothy Bradshaw
From: Miranda Hobbs
Subject: Newbridge Flea Market
Date: 19th July

Introduction
The aim of this report is to describe Newbridge Flea Market and assess its suitability for a shopping trip.

Facilities
Newbridge Flea Market is ideally located near the central train and bus stations in the heart of the town. **Moreover/Yet**, there is a very large car park only a hundred metres away which caters for coaches. There are all sorts of restaurants and snack bars in the streets near the market. Some of the best cafés in town are inside the market area itself. **Although/However**, the streets are quite narrow and crowded and sometimes there are pickpockets.

Shops and prices
There are 150 shops and stalls in Newbridge Flea Market that sell a variety of products from antiques, old coins and stamps, to second-hand clothes and jewellery. **In addition/Yet**, this flea market is well known for its music shops and many musicians go there to pick up second-hand instruments. **Although/Besides** most products are sold at very reasonable prices, the cafés and restaurants tend to be expensive.

Recommendation
In conclusion, Newbridge Flea Market is ideally located and has something to offer everyone. **Although/However** the market area could do with some more security, I think it is an extremely pleasant place to go shopping.

Introduction (Para 1)
State purpose & content of report

(Para 2) ....
....
....
....

(Para 3) ....
....
....
....

Conclusion (Para 5)
Recommendations

b. Complete the table below.

We use *moreover, besides* and .... to add more points to the same topic.
We use *although, yet* and .... to make contrasting points.

c. Complete the paragraph plan.

Linking words
Contrast

3 a. Write sentences as in the example.

1 The staff are friendly. They are very slow.
*The staff are friendly **but** very slow.*
***Although** he staff are friendly, they are very slow.*
*The staff are friendly. **However**, they are very slow.*
*The staff are friendly, **yet** they are very slow.*

2 The supermarket has a car park. It is very expensive.

3 The café is clean and tidy. It is badly ventilated.

Addition

b. Write sentences as in the example.

1 The shops in the village are quite expensive. They do not offer a wide range of products.
*The shops in the village are quite expensive. **Moreover/In addition**, they do not offer a wide range of products.*

2 When you buy things from charity shops you get great bargains. You help people in need.

3 That electrical store has a large variety of items. It offers great discounts.

Build your vocabulary
Opposites

4 a. Choose words from the box to fill in the gaps below.

| • empty • low • rude • wide |

1 friendly ≠ .... staff
2 .... ≠ limited variety
3 high ≠ .... prices
4 .... ≠ crowded place

b. Now use five of the collocations above in sentences of your own.

Recommending

5 Study the examples in the box, then write sentences, as in the example.

I would recommend visiting the local market for a shopping trip.
I would advise you to visit the local market for a shopping trip.
The local market would be suitable for a shopping trip.

1 I would recommend choosing Secrets nightclub for a night out.
2 The Lake District would be suitable for a weekend break.

Your turn

6 Underline the key words in the rubric, then answer the questions.

- The editor of the travel magazine you work for has asked you to write a report assessing the good and bad points of a supermarket in your town. Write your report, describing the facilities, products, service and prices. Recommend the place. (100-120 words)

1 What is the aim of the report?
2 Which subheadings could you use?
   A Products & Prices   D Quality
   B Facilities & Service   E Recommendation
   C Introduction
3 Use the phrases to talk about the supermarket.

Products: wide/disappointing/great/limited/poor variety of products, frozen food, fresh fruit/vegetables, imported/local products
Service: good/excellent/slow/fast, friendly/helpful staff
Prices: resonable, expensive, overpriced, high, low, great/poor value
Facilities: large/small car park, clean/dirty toilets, good/poor/no baby changing facilities, coffee shop, café, seating area

7 Organise your answers under the subheadings, then write your report. You can use the report in Ex. 2 as a model.

43

Happy Days!

1 17/3 St. Patrick's Day (Ireland)

2 5/11 Guy Fawkes Day (UK)

3 1/11 Day of the Dead (Mexico)

4 5/4 Pure Brightness Day (China)

Vocabulary Practice

Celebrations

1 a. Match the celebrations (1-4) to what people do (a-d). Then complete the sentences (1-4) below, as in the example.

a. dress up as skeletons, parade through town, decorate graveyards
b. wear shamrocks, cook traditional dishes, watch street theatre performances
c. set off fireworks, light bonfires, throw Guy Fawkes dummies onto the bonfire
d. go for walks in the countryside, fly kites

1 On 1st November *people in Mexico celebrate the Day of the Dead. They dress up as skeletons, parade through the town and decorate the graveyards.*
2 On 5th April ....
3 On 17th March ....
4 On 5th November ....

b. Now write about a celebration in your country.

On .... people in my country celebrate ....
They ....

Feelings

2 How do these people (1-6) feel? Complete the bubbles.

1. I'm getting married next week! I'm really n _ _ _ _ _ _ _ _ !

2. I can't believe Chloe is getting married! I'm so s _ _ _ _ _ _ _ _ _ !

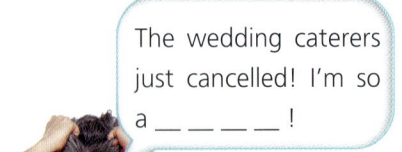

3. The wedding caterers just cancelled! I'm so a _ _ _ _ _ _ !

4. All the family talk about these days is the wedding. I'm really b _ _ _ _ _ !

5. Chloe didn't invite me to her wedding. I'm so d _ _ _ _ _ _ _ _ _ _ _ _ _ !

6. Chloe asked me to be her bridesmaid! I'm really e _ _ _ _ _ _ _ !

6

Greetings/Wishes

3 Match the greetings cards to the occasions.

1 Best wishes for a speedy recovery
2 Good Luck
3 Happy silver anniversary!
4 Congratulations
5 Wishing you love and happiness

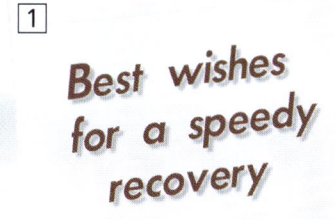

A a couple has just got married
B a friend has just been promoted
C a friend is in hospital
D a friend is taking his exams
E your parents have been married for 25 years

Words often confused

4 Complete the sentences with the words below.

• celebration • reception • festival

1 They had a party in .... of their tenth wedding anniversary.
2 I am really looking forward to the European Film .... at the end of the month.
3 Tina's wedding .... took place in a restaurant in the city centre.

Word formation: nouns

We can add **-ance**, **–tion** and **–ment** to some verbs to form nouns that refer to actions, processes or states.

5 Use the endings **-ance**, **–tion**, **–ment** to make nouns from the following words. Then, check the spelling in your dictionaries.

enjoy ....
celebrate ....
perform ....
decorate ....
amaze ....
compete ....
engage ....
ignore ....

1 The little girl stared at the pumpkin lantern in ....
2 We would like to invite you to our .... party.
3 The musician gave an amazing .... on stage!
4 Sarah and Jim put up all the .... on the Christmas tree.
5 Ronaldo won first prize in the dance ....

6 Complete the missing words in sentences 1-5. Use the pictures to help you.

1 A h................ is a symbol of good luck at weddings.
2 On Christmas Day many people all over the world exchange g................ .
3 The children lit some very spooky Halloween l................ in the front yard!
4 A Christmas s................ is a long sock that children hang up on Christmas Eve.
5 People all over the world celebrate Carnival with p................ in the streets.

45

6

Grammar in Use

Exploring grammar: Future forms

1 Read the dialogue and answer the questions 1-5.

Mum, will you lend me £40 to buy a ticket for the Rockwave Music Festival?

Come on Mum! I'm 16. I'm not a baby anymore! I'll even give you a call when I get there.

Tom and Jessica are going to get tickets tomorrow and they're getting one for me. This time next Saturday I'll be dancing to my favourite rock tunes. Case closed!

That's out of the question! You are not going to that Festival. I won't let you and that's that!

The answer is still no!

Case closed, wallet closed!

1 Look at the highlighted phrase. Which tense is used? Why? How do we form this tense?
2 *Will you lend me …, I won't let you:* What does *will* express in each one?
3 *… are going to get tickets tomorrow … .* Which tense is used? Why? How do we form this tense?
4 *They're getting one for me … .* Explain the use of the present continuous in this sentence.
5 *… when I get there:* Explain the use of the present simple. With what other words do we use the present simple instead of a future form?

Will/Going to

2 Fill in: *will* or *going to*.

1 I'm hungry. I think I .... have a sandwich.
2 The door is open. I .... close it.
3 Oh no! It's already 5 o'clock. We .... to be late.
4 We've decided to throw a party. We .... invite all our friends.
5 I think I .... stay at home tonight.
6 John .... give me a lift to the airport, thanks.

3 What are these people going to do? Look at the pictures and the prompts and write sentences.

- go fishing • take a picture
- blow the candles out
- swim • have a baby

1 She is going to have a baby.

Future continuous

4 Patrick and Fay are organising their summer school's farewell party which is taking place tomorrow night. Look at their list for tomorrow and write sentences.

To Do List

Time	Patrick	Fay
12.00	speak to DJ	decorate the assembly hall
14.00	–	prepare the snacks
16.00	put up the decorations	
18.00	blow up the balloons	test the music

At 12:00 tomorrow Patrick will be speaking to the DJ.

46

Present simple or will

5 Fill in the gaps with the *present simple* or the *future simple* form of the verbs in brackets.

1. As soon as I .... (get) home, I .... (give) you a call.
2. Tommy .... (go) to the park after he .... (finish) his homework.
3. When you .... (clean) the room, Sheila .... (put) up the decorations.

Phrasal verbs: break

6 Choose the correct particle.

1. With this discovery, the young scientists believe they are going to break **out/through** into the commercial market.
2. Nancy broke **down/off** when she heard the news of the accident.
3. Clara broke **in/off** in the middle of her sentence and left the room.
4. The thief broke **away/off** from the police officer and rushed out of the building.
5. A fire broke **out/down** in the shopping centre last night.

Question tags

7 What might you say to somebody in these situations? Use appropriate question tags.

1. You read an exciting novel.
   That novel was exciting, wasn't it?
2. You are not sure, but you think your national football team won.
   Our national ....
3. You think Charlie has never been to the Edinburgh Festival.
   Charlie ....
4. You think your new boss treats people well.
   Our new ....
5. You invite your friends to the cinema.
   Let's ....
6. Ask your dad to answer the phone.
   Dad, answer ....

Sentence transformations

8 Complete the second sentence so that it means the same as the first. Use no more than three words.

1. What are your plans for this weekend?
   What .... to do this weekend?
2. She booked a flight to the Bahamas for next week.
   This time next week she .... to the Bahamas.
3. Call me when you get back from work.
   As soon .... back from work, give me a call.
4. Ellie and James aren't seeing each other anymore.
   Ellie and James .... up.
5. Why don't we go out tonight?
   Let's go .... we?

Prepositional phrases

9 Study the table. Then fill in the blanks with the correct expressions.

on time: when someone is **on time**, he/she arrives at the right time.
in no time: if something happens **in no time** it happens immediately or very quickly
at times: sometimes
at any time: at any moment

1. Don't worry. I'm sure you'll feel better .... at all!
2. The exam starts at 9 in the morning so make sure to be there ....
3. If you need any help with your project, you can call me ....
4. His job is so stressful that .... he wants to quit.

6 Reading

1 a. Which of the following are usually short informative messages? Tick (✓) the correct answers.

1. notices/flyers ✓
2. newspaper articles ☐
3. memos/notes ☐
4. labels ☐
5. emails ☐
6. cards/postcards ☐
7. application letters ☐

b. Circle the correct words that describe this type of message. You may choose more than one in each case.

1. **brief** / long / full text
2. **clear** / **detailed** / unrelated information
3. formal / **informal** / **chatty** style

2 Look at the texts in Ex. 3. What can confuse you in an exercise like this?

- There are unknown words in the text.
- Some words (such as verbs and articles) are omitted.
- The statements do not use words from the text.

3 a. Look at the text in each question (1-5). What does it say? Choose the correct letter *A*, *B* or *C*.

What's on? [1] Tonight, at the local harbour, polka by the sea! Four hours of non-stop dancing to polka music after which you may never want to go near an accordion again!

A The music at the event may not be good.
B You will dance a lot at this event.
C You are not allowed to go near the accordions.

A The Local Puppetry Festival does not occur every year.
B The Local Puppetry Festival doesn't always take place in spring.
C This email refers to an international event.

[2] To: Jonathan Sleigh
From: Sue Shelley
Re: Local Puppetry Festival

In the ad please mention that the Local Puppetry Festival is held in the spring of every odd year. Cheers!

NOW SHOWING [3]
The Glass Menagerie by Tennessee Williams at the **KING'S THEATRE**
Mon 11th – Sat 23rd August (except Sunday 17th) at 7.30pm
Matinees Thu 14th & Sat 16th at 2.00pm

A There aren't any shows in the afternoon.
B On Sunday 17th there is a show at 7.30pm.
C There are shows in the afternoon on specific days.

A If you want to help, call (0207) 976 3330.
B If you want to help, write your name.
C If you come to the bazaar, the school will appreciate it.

[4] Dear class,
Don't forget the school Christmas Charity Bazaar on Saturday! If you want to help out, please sign up, and for any donations please contact Martin on (0207) 976 3330.
Many thanks,
Mr Bloom

Orlando Jazz Festival [5]
Saturday, 15th Nov 6PM
Lake Eola Amphitheatre
Sponsors:
• 'Fresh' Magazine • The Orlando News
• Music Café • Bayne's Supermarket

A The Orlando Jazz Festival sponsors the Music Café and the Orlando News.
B The Orlando Jazz Festival is going to take place at the Music Café and the Orlando News.
C The Music Café and the Orlando News sponsor the Orlando Jazz Festival.

b. Answer the questions (1-3).

1. Which texts (1-5) inform you about the venue of an event?
2. Which texts ask you to pay attention to an important piece of information?
3. Which text asks for your own contribution?

4 Read text 3 in Ex. 3 and send a text message no more than 60 characters long to your friend who would be very interested in going.

48

6

Listening & Speaking

1 🎧 You will hear people speaking in four different situations. For each question put a tick (✓) in the correct box.

1 How many gifts has Jim received?

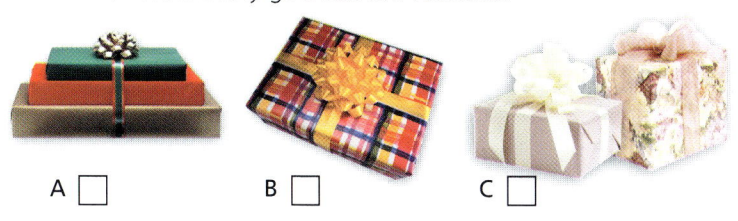

A ☐   B ☐   C ☐

2 Who does Mark invite?

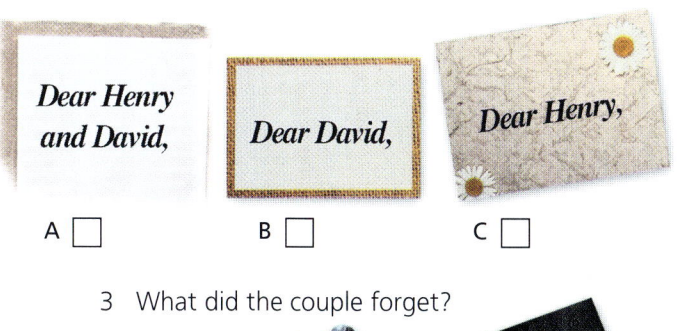

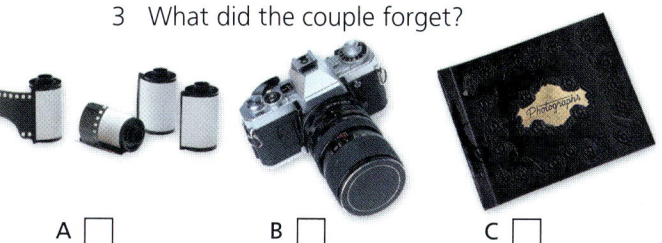

A ☐   B ☐   C ☐

3 What did the couple forget?

A ☐   B ☐   C ☐

4 Which lantern did Rachel make?

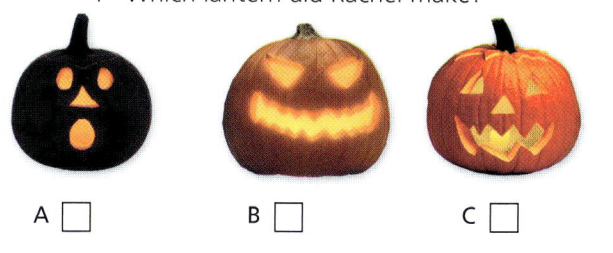

A ☐   B ☐   C ☐

At a party

2 a. Match the items in column A with the ones in column B to form phrases.

A
1 Would you like
2 Yes,
3 Thank you for
4 What a
5 You're
6 Yes,

B
- indeed!
- a lovely evening.
- a second helping?
- please.
- welcome.
- wonderful party!

b. Write short exchanges with the phrases above. Use your own ideas as well.

A: *Would you like* **a second helping**?
B: *Yes, please.*

Gossiping

3 a. Read the first exchange. What do you think went wrong at the wedding? Read through and check.

> A: So, did you go to John and Cathy's wedding?
> B: No, I couldn't make it, but I have first hand information that it was terrible.
> A: Terrible? Really? Tell me all about it!
> B: Well, first of all, I heard that it started pouring down. The ceremony was outdoors so everyone hurried to the reception.
> A: Was the reception nice, at least?
> B: Far from it! A little bird told me that the room was crowded, there was no air-conditioning and what's more, there wasn't enough food!
> A: Come off it!
> B: No it's true! To make matters worse, some of the bride's relatives started a fight!
> A: No, I can't believe that!
> B: Well, apparently, the bride got upset and had a panic attack! I'm telling you ... the whole thing was a complete disaster!

b. Look at the tables. Then, find similar phrases in the dialogue to complete them.

speaker A

Gossiping
- Have you heard...?
- Someone said that ...
- A little bird told me ...
- By the way, did you know that ...
- ...
- ...

speaker B

Expressing Surprise
- Are you sure?
- No way!
- ...
- ...
- ...

c. Use the prompts below to gossip to your best friend about a party you heard was a disaster. Use phrases from the tables above.

- food cold • music boring
- everyone was badly dressed
- some of the guests had a fight

49

6

Writing (an article describing a festival you attended)

Getting started

1 Read the rubric and underline the key words. Then answer the questions (1-3).

> You work for a travel magazine and your boss has asked you to write an article about a festival you have been to. Write your article describing the events and how you felt.

1 What is the purpose of this article?
2 How many paragraphs should it have?
3 What should each paragraph be about?

Let's look closer

2 a. Read the article and complete the paragraph plan.

A FLORAL FEAST

1 ▶ The Toowoomba Carnival of Flowers is the most important floral event in Queensland, Australia. It takes place every year in late September, and it lasts 10 days. Lots of people attend it so last year I decided to go and see what it was all about.

2 ▶ The carnival began with a competition for the best garden in town. After that, there was a spectacular street parade of convertible cars covered in flowers! Then followed a procession of pipers, dressed in traditional Scottish tartan kilts and groups of dancers, wearing bright costumes. Finally, there was the Flower Queen Contest, in which people voted for the most beautiful girl of the day!

3 ▶ I enjoyed every second of this cheerful floral feast. I relaxed walking through the beautiful parks and gardens. I was stunned by the street parade and I had a lot of fun voting for the queen in the contest. On the whole, it was an amazing event.

4 ▶ As I was leaving Toowoomba I felt really sad that the event was over. I couldn't help thinking how much fun I'd had. So, if you ever plan a trip to Toowoomba, try not to miss the lively events and the cheerful atmosphere of this exciting festival.

Introduction
(Para 1) *name, place, time*

(Para 2) ....
....
....

(Para 3) ....
....
....

Conclusion
(Para 4) *feelings & recommendation*

b. Read the article again and find words or phrases describing:

People's clothes: ....
Decorations: ....
Activities: ....
Feelings: ....

Order of Adjectives

3 Put the adjectives in the correct order to complete the sentences.

opinion →	size/length/height →	colour →	origin →	material →	purpose →	noun
a lovely	small	red	Spanish	leather	evening	bag

1 It's a(n) .... costume. (carnival, Italian, nice)
2 It's a(n) .... lantern. (paper, beautiful, Halloween)
3 It's a(n) .... (enormous, ice, impressive) sculpture.
4 It's a(n) .... (cotton, lovely, Moroccan) hat.
5 It's a(n) .... festival. (colourful cheerful, art).

Recommending

4 a. How does the writer recommend the Toowoomba Carnival of Flowers? Which paragraph contains this information?

b. Use expressions from the box below to give your opinion about:
- a film festival you found rather boring
- a concert you really enjoyed

Positive comments
Try not to miss it.
Make sure you don't miss it.
It's a must.
It's definitely worth a visit.

Negative comments
Don't bother with this festival.
Give it a miss.
It's more trouble than it's worth.
It's not worth the ticket price.

Your turn

5 a. Use expressions from the useful language box in the opposite column to answer questions (1-6).

1 What is the name of the most bizarre festival you have ever been to? What was it about?
2 When and where does/did it take place?
3 What were the most important events of the festival?
4 Did people wear any special costumes? Did they eat any special food?
5 How did you feel?
6 Would you recommend this festival?

Useful language
describing events

Occasion: carnival, parade, reception, party, ceremony, celebration, arts festival, religious festival
Location: The ... took place in ... which is located/situated …
Decorations: flowers, paper lanterns, ice sculptures, spectacular paintings, handicrafts, etc.
Activities: crowds dancing/cheering/ clapping/ singing, art/book/ flower exhibitions, street performances, firework displays, craft markets, sporting events, fun fair, etc.
Costumes: traditional/unusual costumes, dazzling colours, funny hats, colourful scarves, national emblems, etc.

b. Read the rubric, and underline the key words. Use your answers to the questions in Ex. 5a to write your article.

- You recently attended a bizarre local festival. Write an article for the school magazine about it. Write when and where it takes places then describe the festival activities. Recommend it to the readers (100-120 words).

51

Eating out!

Vocabulary Practice

Cooking methods

1 Make adjectives from the following verbs. Then, look at the pictures and use the adjectives to fill in the blanks.

1	to fry	*fried*	6	to roast	....
2	to mash	....	7	to scramble	....
3	to steam	....	8	to bake	....
4	to boil	....	9	to stuff	....
5	to grill	....	10	to toast	....

| 1 .... sandwich | 3 .... avocados | 5 .... potato | 7 .... vegetables |
| 2 .... chicken | 4 .... turkey | 6 .... tuna steaks | 8 .... egg |

2 Complete the recipe extracts below. Use the verbs in the list. What dishes do you think they are?

• peel • sprinkle • boil • pour • fry • drain

A *First,* **1)** .... *the potatoes and slice them into long strips. Then,* **2)** .... *them in a deep pan of cooking oil for ten minutes.*

B **3)** .... *the pasta for 8 minutes, then* **4)** .... *the water and* **5)** .... *the tomato sauce over the pasta. Finally,* **6)** .... *some grated Parmesan cheese on top.*

In the supermarket

3 Look at Elaine's shopping basket and write which section she got each item from.

She got the milk from the Dairy Products section.

Food idioms

4 Match the expressions in the box with the following situations.

- It will give him food for thought.
- He's got a sweet tooth.
- He's got a lot on his plate.
- It's a piece of cake.

1 He doesn't find riding difficult.
   ....
   ....
   ....

2 He loves cakes and sugary snacks.
   ....
   ....

3 He's very busy with work and family these days.
   ....
   ....

4 This book will give him a lot of new ideas to think about.
   ....
   ....

52

Food and tastes

5 Fill in the gaps with the right words.

1. If you add **lemon** to your soup, it makes it taste s............... .
2. Tina added some **chilli peppers** to the pasta sauce to make it s............... .
3. This ice cream is very s............... with all that **syrup** on top.
4. My coffee is b...............! Pass me the **sugar**, please.
5. This soup has too much **salt** in it! I can't eat something that s...............!

Quantities of food

6 a. Fill in: *pot*, *handful*, *clove*, *bar*, *pinch*.

1. Sprinkle a .... of chopped nuts on top and serve.
2. Could you pass me that .... of chocolate, please?
3. Add a .... of salt and pepper to the sauce.
4. There's only one .... of yoghurt left in the fridge.
5. We need a .... of garlic for this recipe.

b. Make spidergrams for each of the prompts, then make sentences, as in the example.

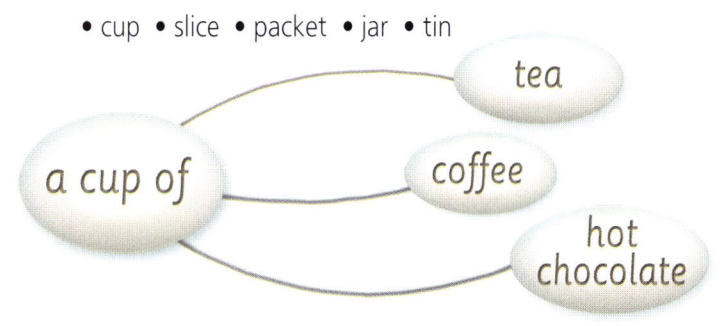

• cup • slice • packet • jar • tin

a cup of — tea
a cup of — coffee
a cup of — hot chocolate

I always have a cup of coffee first thing in the morning.

Cutlery and crockery

7 Underline the odd one out. Explain your choice.

1. tray, cooker, toaster, mixer
2. plate, saucer, soup bowl, blender
3. tablespoon, carving knife, serving dish, dessert fork
4. glass, mug, kettle, jug

Word formation: nouns

We use **-er, -or, -ist** to form nouns referring to people who do a particular kind of work. eg *a sing**er** is someone who sings for a living*

8 Use *-er, -or, -ist* to make nouns from the following verbs. Then, make sentences using the nouns.

translate ....
art ....
act ....
biology ....
piano ....
conduct ....
write ....
paint ....

A translator is a person who translates texts or speech from one language to another.

Words often confused

9 Match the words (1-4) with their definitions (a-d). Then, underline the correct word in the sentences 1-4.

1) receipt	a) a person whose job it is to prepare and cook food	●●●●○ N-COUNT = chef	
2) recipe	b) a list of ingredients and a set of instructions that tell you how to cook something	●●○○○ N-COUNT	
3) cook	c) a large metal device for cooking food using gas or electricity	●○○○○ N-COUNT	
4) cooker	d) a piece of paper that you get from someone as proof that they have received money from you, usually in a shop when you buy something	●●○○○ N-COUNT	

1. He bought a brand new **cook/cooker**.
2. When you pay at the counter, always ask the shop assistant for a **recipe/receipt**.
3. Tim is such a wonderful **cooker/cook**.
4. This is a traditional **recipe/receipt** for chocolate biscuits.

7

Grammar in Use

Exploring grammar: Past perfect & Past perfect continuous

1 Read the dialogue and answer the questions (1-3).

Ann: Hey, do you want some of this delicious brownie? It's homemade.
Bill: I'm tempted, but I'm not allowed to have any.
Ann: What do you mean you are not allowed?
Bill: Well, there are a few walnuts on top and it has a little cream in it and I am allergic to both of them. The last time I had a brownie I ended up in hospital.
Ann: How come?
Bill: *Well, minutes after I had finished the brownie, I had difficulty breathing.* I had been coughing for half an hour, so David took me to the hospital. *By the time I reached the hospital, my tongue had swollen up.*
Ann: It sounds terrible! So what are you supposed to do from now on?
Bill: Avoid mouth-watering brownies like the one you are eating right now!

1 Look at the sentences in italics. How many actions took place? Which is the one that happened first and which is the one that followed? Which tense is the first one in and which tense is the second one in?

2 Find a past perfect continuous verb form in the dialogue. What are the time expressions used with this tense?

3 Read the dialogue and underline the quantifiers that go with countable nouns and the quantifiers that go with uncountable nouns. Which quantifiers go with both?

Past perfect/Past perfect continuous

2 a. Put the verbs in brackets into the *past perfect simple* or *past perfect continuous*.

1 When she tasted the soup, she realised she .... (add) sugar instead of salt!
2 An hour passed before we realised that we .... (forget) to turn on the oven!
3 Sheila .... (already/add) three spoons of sugar to Jim's coffee when she remembered that he used artificial sweetener.
4 Tony .... (cook) since 10 o'clock for the party when there was a power cut.
5 Grandma .... (read) her book for an hour when she smelt something burning.

b. Write a short paragraph about a kitchen disaster you had. Use the prompts below to help you.

• cut • drop • forget • spill • burn

Quantifiers

3 Read the food facts below, then circle the correct word in bold.

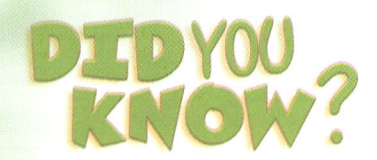

DID YOU KNOW?

1 Cola **is/are** made from the kola nut.
2 **Much/Many** frozen vegetables **have/has** more vitamins than fresh ones that are over five days old.
3 When flour **is/are** properly stored, it will keep for six to eight months.
4 A glass of red wine a day **help/helps** to protect against heart disease.
5 Chocolate **contain/contains** caffeine.
6 The avocado **is/are** a vegetable, but we use it as a fruit.

4 Use *how much/ how many* to ask questions. Then, use *a few/a little* to answer them.

1 salt/you put in/soup?
   How much salt did you put in the soup?
   Just a little.
2 bananas/you get/yesterday?
3 sugar/you take/coffee?
4 milk/you drink/every day?
5 burgers/you eat/last night?

54

5 Look at the picture and make sentences with *some/any*. Use the prompts.

- turkey • strawberries
- bowls • glasses • grapes
- lettuce • soup • tomatoes
- bread • water

There is some turkey. There aren't any strawberries.

Every/any/no

6 Use *some/any/no/every* + *body/thing/where* to complete the sentences below.

1 It's too hot in here. Let's go *somewhere* cool.
2 All the guests have gone home. There's .... here but me.
3 I'm going to the supermarket. Is there .... you need?
4 The party was a huge sucess! .... went according to plan!
5 This lesson is very important! Can I have .... attention please?
6 I've got .... in my eye! It really stings.
7 The people around me are strangers. I don't know ....
8 Can I please stay at your place? I have .... else to go.

Phrasal verbs: give

7 Choose the correct particle.

1 A: I heard Ann's buying a new sofa.
   B: Really? Will she be giving **away/out** the old one then?
2 A: I can't believe you give **out/off** your telephone number so easily.
   B: Oh come on. It's only a telephone number.
3 A: It was nice of him to give **up/in** his seat, wasn't it?
   B: Yes, it was very kind indeed.
4 A: Come on, James! Stop arguing. You know you are wrong.
   B: OK, then. I give **in/off**.
5 A: Don't forget to give me **back/away** that CD.
   B: Sure. I'll come round with it next week.

Prepositions

8 Choose expressions from the box to fill in the gaps.

> If someone or something is **on the way**, they will arrive soon.
> If someone or something is **in the way**, they prevent you from moving forward or seeing clearly.
> You say **by the way** when you add something to what you are saying, especially something that you have just thought of.

1 Don't worry sir, your dinner is ....
2 My holiday starts next week! .... , do you have any holiday plans?
3 Excuse me, madam. I can't see the screen. Your head is ....

Sentence transformations

9 Complete the second sentence so that it means the same as the first. Use no more than three words.

1 Let's go to a nice, relaxing place to eat.
   Let's go .... and relaxing to eat.
2 Sam called the restaurant and reserved a table.
   Sam reserved a table after .... the restaurant.
3 We have run out of salt!
   There .... salt left.
4 She doesn't eat fatty foods any more because she wants to lose weight!
   She gave .... foods to lose weight.
5 There isn't much milk in the fridge.
   There is only .... in the fridge.

55

7

Reading

A — Xavier: I enjoy cooking on location. We get to go to lots of different places and sometimes we meet the actors. It can be quite hard work and we do start early, but it's much better than working in an office.

B — Melina: I haven't eaten meat for quite a long time. I mean, I'm not against people eating meat and I occasionally eat fish and chicken, but I do think that hamburgers and junk food are bad for you.

C — Joe: The thought of eating dead animals is disgusting. When I invite people round to my house for dinner, they know I'm going to offer them something different and wholesome at the same time.

D — Kim: My partner and I love going out to eat. There's so much variety on offer around here and we simply haven't got time to cook and wash up afterwards.

E — Soraya: There are some great takeaways near where I live. There's a great Japanese restaurant that does home deliveries and hundreds of Indian restaurants.

F — Matthew: Nothing beats a Sunday roast with my family. There are usually about ten of us around the dining room table and it's nice cooking for everyone.

G — Keanu: We often invite people around for dinner and they say that my wife cooks like a professional. Well, her cooking is amazing, and she has thought about writing a cookery book, but she's too busy with other things at the moment.

1
a. Skim the texts (A-G) and underline the phrases that the people use to express likes or dislikes.

b. Use the expressions to write sentences about your preferences.

I enjoy eating out with friends. It's a good way to have fun.

2 a. Read the texts (A-G) and answer questions 1-6. One of the people is not referred to.

1. Who likes going out to different kinds of restaurants?
2. Who likes his/her partner's cooking?
3. Who doesn't eat meat a lot?
4. Who is a vegetarian?
5. Who likes cooking for his/her family?
6. Who cooks professionally?

b. Which of the people in texts A-G have similar ideas about food?

Decision making

3 Are you happy with your eating habits? What could you do to improve your diet? Use the expressions in the box to make a list of resolutions.

> First thing tomorrow, I will stop …
> From now on, I will cut down on …
> I'm going to avoid …
> I've decided to start …
> I'm never going to eat … again.

First thing tomorrow, I will stop drinking soft drinks.

Listening & Speaking
Giving instructions

1 a. Read the first four lines of the dialogue in Ex. 1b. Where are Pat & Jane? What are they doing? Do you think they can make it? Read and check.

b. Use expressions from the box to complete the dialogue.

Pat: Jane, can you help me, please?
Jane: Sure. What's up?
Pat: Well, I'm trying to make tomato soup, but I'm having trouble following the recipe.
Jane: Let me have a look. Well, 1) .... check that you have got all the ingredients.
Pat: Yes, I know. I've done that.
Jane: Then, 2) .... chop the onions, peppers and tomatoes.
Pat: Right. They're ready.
Jane: 3) .... , you fry the onions and peppers for five minutes.
Pat: OK. Great. What do I do next?
Jane: Well, the next step is to add the tomatoes, some herbs and 12 teaspoons of salt.
Pat: 12 teaspoons? All right – now what?
Jane: Well, 4) .... is pour in the water and let the mixture simmer for half an hour.
Pat: Oh, thanks, Jane. Let's have a little taste … Ugh! It's really salty!
Jane: Oh, dear. Let me check the recipe again … Oh, sorry, Kate. It says ½ teaspoon of salt, not 12 teaspoons!

Giving instructions	
Before you begin, you should …	Once you've done that, …
The first thing you do is …	When you finish that, …
The next step is to …	In the end, …
	The last thing you do is …

c. Work in pairs. Use the language in the box to act out a similar dialogue, giving instructions on how to boil an egg. Give your dialogue an unexpected ending.

Leaving messages

2 a. You will hear a chef leaving a telephone message for a fruit and vegetable supplier. Look at the gaps (1-6). Which ask for a number? Now, listen and fill in the missing information on the invoice.

INVOICE

FROM	Fisher's Organic Fruit & Vegetables	N° I320
TO	Oliver Jones / Bay Tree Restaurant	DATE 12 July

ITEM:	QUANTITY:	COST:
Organic carrots: 1) .... kg		£ 8.00
Baby onions: 2) .... boxes		£ 14.50
Cooking 3) .... : 2 crates		£ 11.00
Wild mushrooms: 3 kg		£ 4) ....
Garden lettuce: 5) .... boxes		£ 9.90
Blood oranges: 5 kg		£ 3.00
Aubergines: 6) .... kg		£ 15.00
	TOTAL	£ 261.40

b. Listen to the recording again. Which vegetables does the chef still need?

Describing a picture

3 Describe the picture. Talk about:

- where the people are
- how they are related to each other
- what each of them is doing
- how they feel

57

7

Writing (a thank-you email)

Getting started

1 Read the rubric and underline the key words. Then answer the questions.

> You went on a picnic your neighbour organised last Saturday. Write a thank-you email to your neighbour. In your email you should:
> - thank her for a wonderful afternoon
> - say what you enjoyed the most (dishes)
> - invite her to a garden party at your place next weekend

1 What is the purpose of the email?
2 What tenses should you use?
3 Think of some phrases you could use to: a) express your thanks: b) invite your neighbour to the party.

Let's look closer

2 a. Read the email below and complete the paragraph plan.

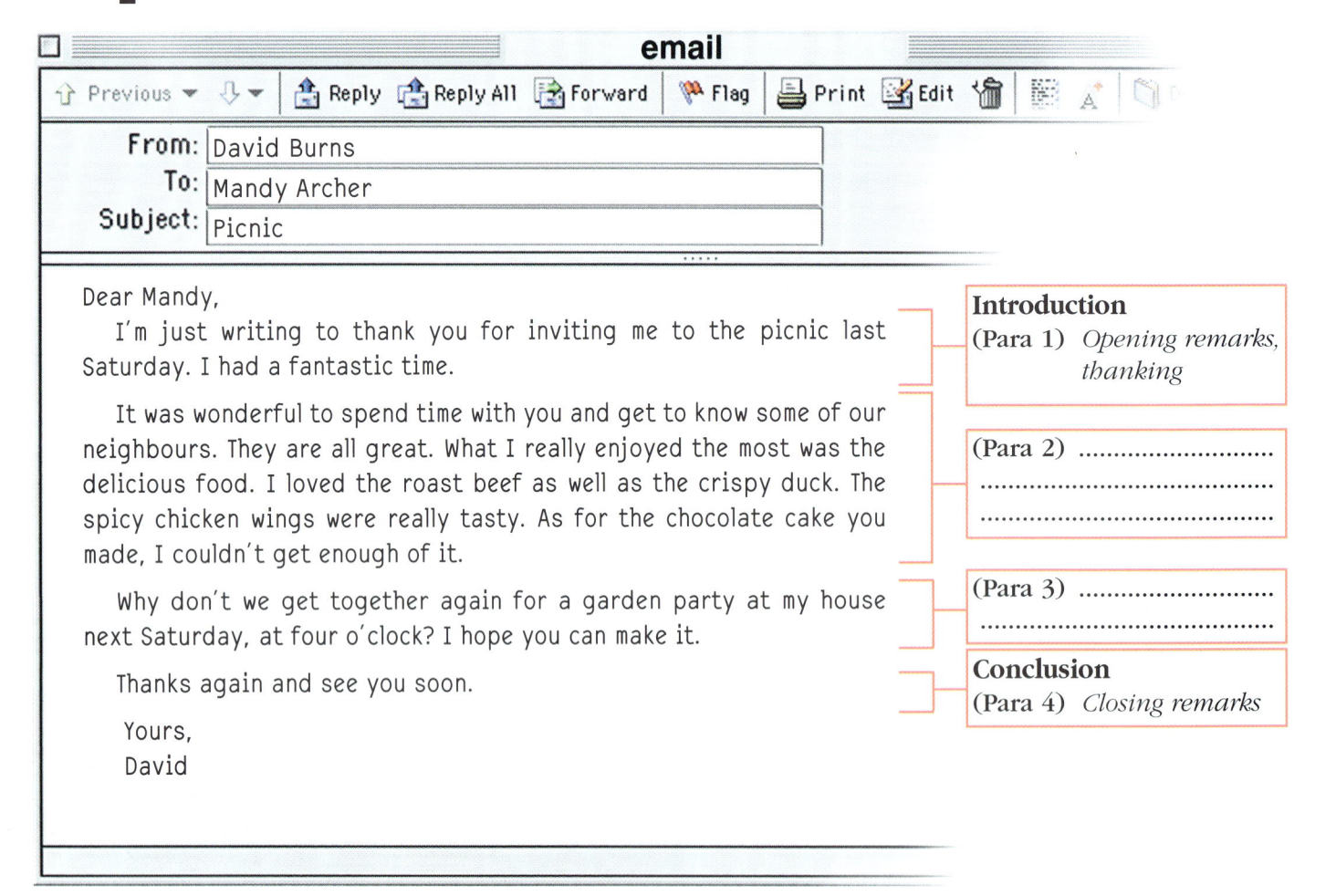

---

email

From: David Burns
To: Mandy Archer
Subject: Picnic

Dear Mandy,

I'm just writing to thank you for inviting me to the picnic last Saturday. I had a fantastic time.

It was wonderful to spend time with you and get to know some of our neighbours. They are all great. What I really enjoyed the most was the delicious food. I loved the roast beef as well as the crispy duck. The spicy chicken wings were really tasty. As for the chocolate cake you made, I couldn't get enough of it.

Why don't we get together again for a garden party at my house next Saturday, at four o'clock? I hope you can make it.

Thanks again and see you soon.

Yours,
David

Introduction
(Para 1) *Opening remarks, thanking*

(Para 2) ....
....
....

(Para 3) ....
....

Conclusion
(Para 4) *Closing remarks*

b. Read the email again and underline the phrases used: to express thanks; to invite.

c. Which words/phrases in the email express David's feelings?

58

Expressing thanks

3 a. Which of the following can you thank someone for?

- help • happiness • generosity • memory
- excitement • effort • kindness
- amazement • willingness • impression
- honesty • sensitivity • ambition

b. Use phrases from the useful language box as well as nouns from Ex. 3a to rewrite the following sentences (1-5), as in the example.

Useful language — expressing thanks

Thanks a million for …
A big thank-you for …
Special thanks for …
Last but not least, thanks to …
Once again, thanks for …

1. You were very helpful at my dinner party.
   Thank you for your help at my dinner party.
2. You were very kind on my first day at work.
3. You were very generous during my stay at your holiday house.
4. You tried very hard to make the evening such a success.
5. You were very willing to help me with my project.

Expressing pleasure

4 Use phrases from the useful language box to express your feelings about the following situations (1-3).

Useful language — expressing pleasure

I had a great time/ It was so lovely of you …
I enjoyed your hospitality …
It gave me great pleasure …
I was impressed with …

1. Your neighbour invited you to a garden party.
2. Your colleague invited you to a dinner party at his house.
3. Your neighbour invited your children to her son's birthday party.

Your turn

5 Read the rubric and underline the key words. Then answer questions 1-4.

> Write a short email to thank your friend for the wonderful dinner party you attended at his/her place last weekend. In your letter you should:
> - thank him/her for the lovely evening
> - say what you liked the most (dishes, atmosphere)
> - invite him/her to a barbecue at your house next weekend

Food: tasty, delicious, mouthwatering, well cooked
Atmosphere: friendly, relaxing, romantic, great music, etc

1. When did you last go to a dinner party?
2. What was the occasion?
3. Which were the dishes you enjoyed the most?
4. What was the atmosphere like?

6 Use your answers in Ex. 5 to write your email (50-80 words).

59

Fit for Life

Vocabulary Practice

Parts of the body

1 a. Label the parts of the body (1-5) in the picture.

- stomach
- shoulder
- arm
- thigh
- calf

1 ....
2 ....
3 ....
4 ....
5 ....

b. Match the parts of the body in Ex. 1a with the activities that exercise them. Then write sentences, as in the example.

- sit-ups • tennis
- step training
- weight-lifting • cycling

Weight-lifting/Tennis exercises your shoulders.

Qualities

2 What qualities do you need in order to do the sports in the pictures? Write sentences, as in the example.

- courage
- quick reactions
- sense of adventure
- sense of direction
- brave
- fit
- careful

parachuting
snorkelling
cycling
skiing

*You need to be **brave** to go parachuting. You also need to have a **sense of adventure**.*

Sports Equipment/Sports Places

3 Match the columns. Then write sentences, as in the example.

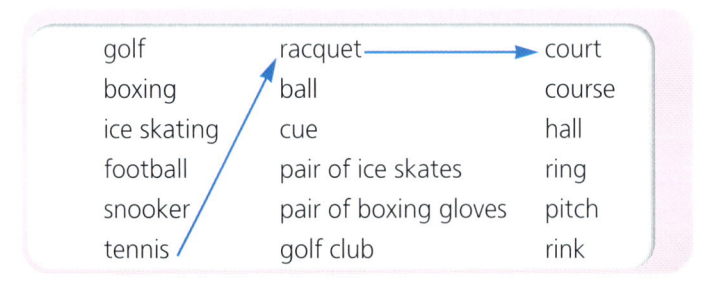

golf	racquet	court
boxing	ball	course
ice skating	cue	hall
football	pair of ice skates	ring
snooker	pair of boxing gloves	pitch
tennis	golf club	rink

To play tennis you need a racquet. You play tennis on a court.

4 Cheryl loves playing sports. Look at the notes and write sentences using **go**, **play** and **do**, as in the example.

jog:	every morning
tennis:	three times a week
ski:	once a month in the winter
gymnastics:	twice a week
swim:	every weekend in the summer

1 *She goes jogging every morning.*
2 ....
3 ....
4 ....
5 ....

60

Injuries

5 Fill in the missing verbs. Then use the sentences to give advice, as in the example.

• rub • put • take • wrap

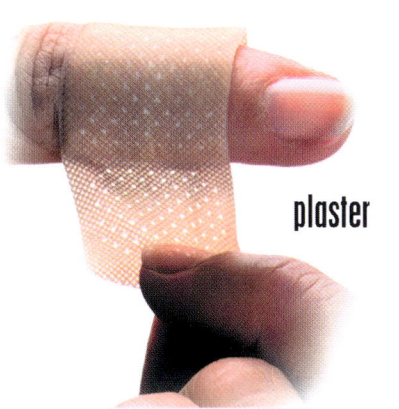

bandage
3 .... around injury to protect and support it.

plaster
1 .... on cut to keep it clean.

antiseptic cream
2 .... gently on injury to prevent infection.

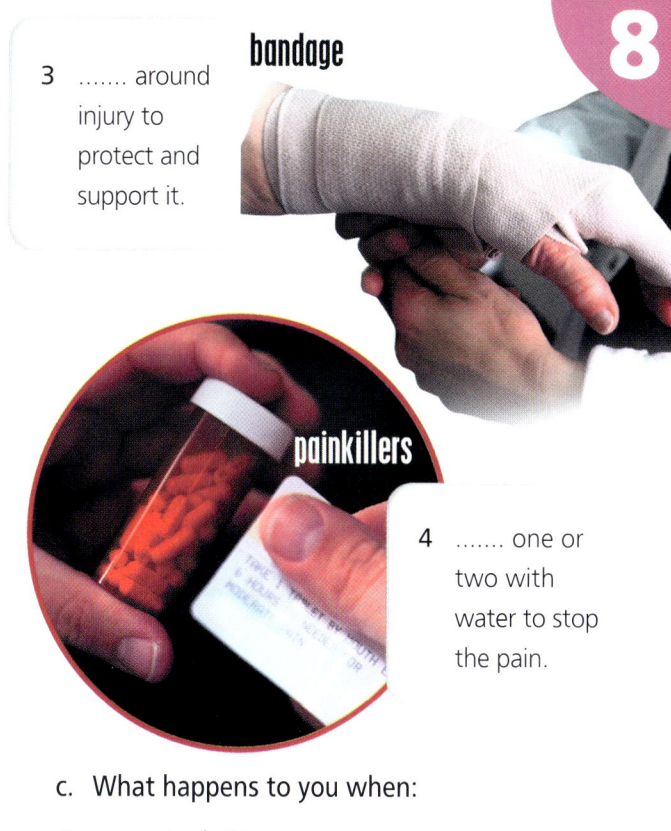

painkillers
4 .... one or two with water to stop the pain.

1 A: *I've hurt my arm.*
   B: *You should wrap a bandage around the injury to protect and support it.*
2 A: I've just cut my finger!
   B: ....
3 A: I have a splitting headache!
   B: ....
4 A: I've hurt my knee!
   B: ....

Describing pain

6 a. Fill in: *ache* or *sore*.

1 tooth ....
2 stomach............
3 .... throat
4 back.................

b. Match column A with column B to form complete sentences.

A
1 My eyes
2 I had a muscle
3 The little boy had a sharp pain
4 Maria had a sore

B
a in his chest and coughed a lot.
b cramp while exercising at the gym.
c ache from staring at the computer screen.
d throat due to a virus.

c. What happens to you when:

1 you eat a lot? ....
2 you lift something heavy suddenly? ....
3 you bite hard on something tough? ....
4 you drink very cold drinks? ....

Word Building: -ful/-less

-ful and *-less* are added to nouns in order to form adjectives which indicate that someone or something *has* (-ful) or *does not have* (-less) the thing which the noun refers to.

7 a. Use *-ful* and *-less* to form adjectives from the following nouns. Explain what they mean.

1 help: *helpful , helpless*
2 taste: ...., ...
3 joy: ...., ...
4 meaning: ...., ...
5 mind: ...., ...
6 care: ...., ...

b. Use words from Ex. 7a to complete the sentences (a-d).

a Steven's crashed his car again! What a .... driver!
b The Irish are .... people who love music and dancing.
c She always wears stylish clothes and .... jewellery.
d Some sentences in this piece of writing are completely ....!

8

Grammar in Use

Exploring Grammar: The passive

1 Read the text and answer the questions.

Sport

Football

Latest Results

Arsenal defeated by Aston Villa (2-1) Chelsea beat Bolton (1-0).
Paul Wilkinson injured during the Chelsea vs. Bolton match. Manchester United are now at the top of the Premiership.

1 Look at the part of the text in italics. Which verb form is active and which is passive?
2 Look at the passive verb form. Is there anything missing? Why?
3 Turn the active sentence into the passive. What differences do you notice?
4 Find another sentence in the passive in the text. Rewrite it including any parts that have been left out.

2 What do the notices mean? Rewrite them as full sentences.

A **Aerobics instructor wanted**

B **Tickets for World Cup sold here!**

C **Changing rooms cleaned daily at noon and before closing.**

D **Purse found yesterday in staff room. Contact Mark in Administration office.**

3 Write complete questions using the prompts. Can you answer them?

OLYMPIC GAMES Quiz

1 Who /modern/Olympic Games/start/by?
....
2 Which sports/include/in every modern Olympics/since 1896?
....
3 Where/next Olympic Games/hold?
....
4 Which sport/play/with a bow and arrow?
....

Conditionals

4 You are a sports instructor at a popular gym. Use the prompts (1-6) to give useful tips to the members.

1 bend knees when lift weights/hurt back
If you don't bend your knees when you lift weights, you will hurt your back.
2 warm up before jogging/strain muscles
3 wear wrong running shoes/injure feet
4 feel tired/stop immediately
5 not drink enough water/become dehydrated
6 need a locker/see receptionist

5 Complete the sentences.

1 If I find your wallet, ...
2 If you take more exercise, ...
3 I'll probably go to the party ....
4 I'll take the job if ....
5 If he calls me, ...

If I find your wallet, I'll give it to you.

Phrasal verbs: bring

6 Join the parts of the sentences.

1	Stella brought ...
2	We talked a lot and she brought ...
3	He brought ...
4	The photographs of us brought ...

a ... back so many nice memories.
b ... out a new book last year.
c ... up the subject of our partnership.
d ... her baby girl round to my place last night.

Sentence transformations

7 Complete the second sentence so that it means exactly the same as the first. Use no more than three words.

1 You can't play ice hockey if you don't have the right equipment.
You can't play ice hockey unless .... the right equipment.

2 The coach will punish any player who doesn't wear his uniform.
Any player who doesn't wear his uniform .... punished by the coach.

3 Wearing the wrong shoes while jogging injures your feet.
If you wear the wrong shoes while jogging, ... injure your feet.

4 All cyclists must wear bicycle helmets.
Bicycle helmets .... by all cyclists.

5 A car crash caused his back injury.
His back injury .... a car crash.

Prepositional Phrases

8 Fill in the gaps with expressions from the box.

- When something, eg. a work of art, is *on view* it is shown to the public.
- To have something *in view* is to plan towards it.
- You use *in my view* when you want to indicate that you are stating a personal opinion.

1 When making the documentary, the director had very clear aims ....
2 A selection of Picasso's sketches will be .... at the museum until September.
3 ...., lots of things in the company will improve soon.

Words with prepositions

9 Fill in: *on*, *into*, *through*, *over*.

1 The athletes are running .... the track.
2 It takes great skill to jump .... hurdles.
3 The woman is diving .... the pool.  
4 They are making their way .... the water.

Error correction

10 Find and correct five mistakes in Tom's note.

Hi Donald,
Don't forget we are playing against Lancing in Saturday. If nothing changes, we would meet outside the stadium at 8.30. If you arrived early, wait for the rest of the team at the gate. Team equipment will be checked from the referee before the game, so make sure everything you need is pack in your bag.
Cheers,
Tom

8

Reading

1 Which is the most important sports venue in your country? Describe it.

2 Skim through the text and find:
- the names of three historic stadiums
- three sporting events a modern stadium can host
- the names of two athletes who made history

3 Read statements 1-10. Say whether they are true *(T)* or false *(F)*.

1 The first stadium was built in 776 BC. ....
2 Wars stopped during the Olympic Games. ....
3 In the past, gladiators used to fight in stadiums. ....
4 Stadiums had not been built before the 19th century. ....
5 Nowadays, only football, baseball and rock concerts are held in stadiums. ....
6 Only football matches were played at Wembley stadium in the past. ....
7 Mark Spitz came first in five different sports. ....
8 Lasse Viren led the 2000m race from the start. ....
9 Many stadiums used to be castles in the past. ....
10 Stadiums are very common in cities nowadays. ....

4 Use your dictionary to find the meanings of the words in bold. Then use them in sentences of your own.

Where History is made

Legend has it that the first sports stadium was built to **hold** the Olympic Games, which were created by the Greeks thousands of years ago. The first recorded date is 776 BC but the stadiums existed before then. Athletes came from many cities to **compete**, and fighting between nations stopped during the games. Stadiums then became part of Greek and Roman culture and thousands of **spectators** often **gathered** to see athletes take part in sporting events or to watch **gladiators** fight.

However, stadiums **disappeared** with the **fall** of the Roman Empire and were not used again until towards the end of the 19th century. Since then, thousands of stadiums have been built in big cities all over the world, and everything from football and baseball games to rock concerts are held in them. They have once again become places where **legends** are created and history is made.

Wembley stadium in London was probably one of the most famous football stadiums in the world. Many great events from the **spectacular** 1966 World Cup to huge pop concerts and **athletics championships** were held there. In 1950, the historic World Cup final between Brazil and Uruguay was played before a **crowd** of 200,000 spectators in the **gigantic** Maracana stadium in Rio de Janeiro. The Olympiastadion in Munich was built for the 1972 Olympic Games which was when the famous swimmer Mark Spitz won seven gold medals and **established** five world records. At the same games, in this stadium Lasse Viren also became a hero. While in fifth place in the 2000m race, he fell to the ground, but got up and **eventually** won a gold medal and set a world record.

Stadiums are now a part of urban life, often standing tall in our cities like majestic castles did in the past.

Listening & Speaking

Making assumptions

1 Look at the picture. Use the phrases in the box and answer the questions.

> **Making assumptions**
> They could be ...; They may be ...; They must/can't be ...; They might/probably have ...; Perhaps, it's ...

1 Who are the people in the picture?
2 Where are they?
3 What are they doing?
4 How do they feel? Why?

Going climbing

2 a. What do you think you need to take with you when you go climbing in the mountains?

b. You will hear someone talking to students about a rock climbing course. Listen and fill in the missing information.

SOC ROCK CLIMBING COURSE

Course cost includes:
- technical climbing gear (harness, helmet, rope)
- 1) .... and transportation
- adult supervision during non-climbing hours
- accommodation at the Newton Inn
- all 2) .... (if you have dietary restrictions, please let us know)

Climbers need to bring:
- backpack or rucksack
- toiletries
- small 3) .... (plasters, tape and bandages)
- a waterproof jacket
- plenty of warm clothes, 4) .... and thermal underwear
- sunscreen, sunglasses and something to protect your head
- two 5) .... of water
- 6) .... and a towel
- £40-£50 pocket 7) ....

Working out

3 a. Read the first exchange in the dialogue in Ex. 3b. Where are Alan and Ben?

b. Read the dialogue. Some phrases have been left out. Use phrases from the list below (A-F) to complete the gaps (1-5). There is one extra phrase you don't need.

Alan: Hi, Ben. Training for the big match?
Ben: Yeah. I've got to stay in shape. I don't want to 1 ☐ .
Alan: Good for you. Don't overdo it, though. You don't want to pull a muscle.
Ben: Don't worry. I know 2 ☐ . Anyway, my personal trainer has told me the exercises to do for the best results.
Alan: A personal trainer, eh? You are going up in the world!
Ben: Yeah. So, are you coming to 3 ☐ ?
Alan: Sure! I wouldn't miss it for the world! You know me – I'm addicted to football.
Ben: Ha ha! Aren't we all?
Alan: Well, I'd better get on with my own workout and let you do yours.
Ben: Thanks, Alan. See you 4 ☐ .
Alan: You bet! Good luck! I hope you win!
Ben: You're not 5 ☐ ! Cheers, Alan.

A at the game   D let the team down
B what I'm doing   E see the match
C the only one   F how to do it

4 Read the dialogue again, then match the sentences (1-6) to the people who might say them.

• Alan • Ben • Ben's personal trainer

1 I don't want to disappoint the other players.
2 Don't exercise too hard.
3 These are the most effective exercises you can do.
4 I'll definitely be at the match.
5 I need to keep fit.
6 I'm crazy about football.

5 In pairs, give the dialogue a different ending.

65

8 Writing (Writing a pros and cons essay)

Let's get started

1 Read the rubric and underline the key words. Brainstorm the positive and negative aspects of exercising indoors and complete the mind maps.

- Your teacher has asked you to write an essay discussing the pros and cons of exercising indoors.

pros — safer

cons — gyms get crowded

Let's look closer

2 a. Read the essay below and complete the paragraph plan. How many of your own ideas have been included in the essay?

b. How does the author feel about exercising indoors? In which paragraph is this mentioned?

1 Exercising is the best way to keep fit and healthy. Most people exercise indoors in a gym or sports centre, but exercising outdoors can be just as effective.

2 There are many advantages to exercising indoors. Firstly, you don't have to worry about the weather. In addition, it's safer to exercise indoors because you don't have to worry about traffic or slippery roads. Furthermore, there are trained professionals to help you so that you don't hurt yourself.

3 However, exercising indoors does have some disadvantages. To start with, you do not get any fresh air inside a gym. Gyms can also get very crowded and you can waste a lot of time waiting to use the equipment. In addition, there aren't many sporting activities you can do.

4 All in all, I believe that exercising outdoors is healthier and a lot more fun. You can do anything from playing football to windsurfing or hiking. In my opinion, most of us spend too much time indoors and even a jog around the park is healthier than being stuck in a stuffy, overcrowded gym.

Introduction
(Para 1) *state the topic*

(Para 2) ....
....
....

(Para 3) ....
....
....

Conclusion
(Para 4) *Sum up & state your opinion*

c. Read the essay again. What are the words the writer has used to:
link similar ideas? ....
link opposing ideas? ....

Linking similar ideas

3 Look at the topic sentence below. Then, use the prompts below to complete the paragraph. Put your arguments in order by using: *to begin with*, *secondly*, *finally*.

There are a number of advantages to doing sports, especially for children. To begin with, ………… .

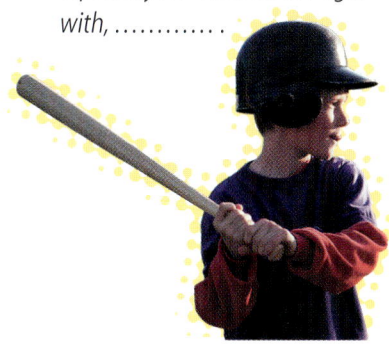

• you can make friends • keep in shape • good for your health

4 Use *what's more*, *also*, *in addition* and the prompts below to write supporting sentences for the following topic sentence.

Professional athletes lead difficult lives.

• follow special diets
• train for many hours a day
• get injured
• have to sleep very early
• career stops in their mid 30s

Linking opposing ideas

5 Use the prompts to develop the following topic sentence into a paragraph. Use *yet*, *however*, *but* or *although*.

Many people believe that watching a football match on TV is better than watching it live.

• feel the excitement
• see all the action
• stadium too crowded
• great atmosphere
• violent episodes

6 Complete the following sentences.

1 Living alone can be very expensive. **However**, ………………………
2 One of the advantages of studying abroad is that you experience another way of life. **What's more**, ……………………………
3 Having a pet at home is very troublesome. **To start with**, …………
………………………………………………………………………… .
4 Travelling by plane is faster, **yet**, ……………………………………… .
5 Life in a big city is very difficult. **First of all**, …………………………… .

Your turn

7 a. Read the rubric and underline the key words.

Your teacher has asked you to write an essay discussing the advantages and disadvantages of team sports. (100-120 words)

b. Sort the ideas below into two categories: **pros** & **cons**. Then, add your own ideas to each category.

• can't exercise whenever you feel like it
• can't exercise at your own pace
• meet new people
• develop team work skills
• playing for victory is more exciting

8 a. Use the prompts above to answer the following questions.

1 Do you and your friends play sports? Why?
2 What are the advantages and disadvantages of playing sports in a team?
3 Do you like playing in a team or do you prefer exercising on your own? Why?

b. Use your answers in Ex. 8a to make a plan of your essay. Use the plan in Ex. 2 as a model. Now write your essay.

67

Going out!

Vocabulary Practice

Forms of entertainment

1 a. Read the extracts A-C. Then, complete the table below.

A

Chapter 2
The phone rang about two o'clock that morning. Mary woke up with a start, and tripped over the cat as she ran downstairs to answer it. 'Who could be calling at this hour?' she wondered.

B

I wandered lonely as a cloud
That floats on high o'er vales and hills,
When all at once I saw a crowd,
A host, of golden daffodils.

C

Chorus
We are the world
We are the children
We are the ones who make a brighter day
So let's start giving

Extract	What is it?	Who wrote it?
A	novel	....
B	poem	....
C	....	a songwriter

b. Use the table to make sentences, as in the example.

Extract A is from a novel. It was written by a novelist.

Jobs in the entertainment industry

2 Write the clues for the crossword.

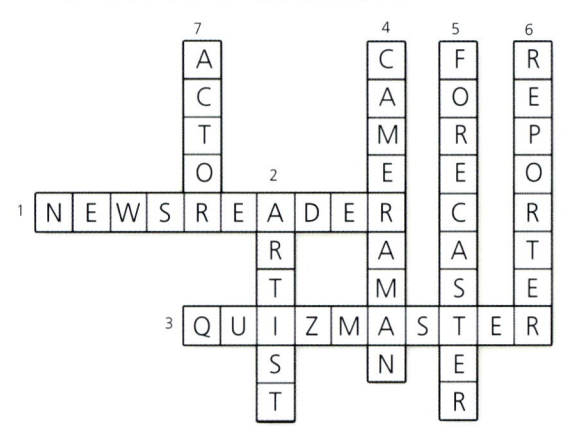

```
        7         4   5   6
        A         C   F   R
        C         A   O   E
        T         M   R   P
        O    2    E   E   O
    1 N E W S R E A D E R   R
              R   A   C   T
              T   M   A   E
          3 Q U I Z M A S T E R
              S       N   E
              T           R
```

1 A *newsreader* is a person who *reads the news on the radio*.
2 A make-up ... is a person who ....
3 A ... is a person who ....
4 A ... is a person who ....
5 A weather ... is a person who ....
6 A ... is a person who ....
7 An ... is a person who ....

Film genres

3 a. Read the excerpts from the following film reviews and say what kind of films they are.

A
The film is praised by critics for its effective combination of ghostly terror and small-town charm ...

B
The songs are terrific and the dancing is brilliant ...

C
Finding Nemo is an exciting aquatic adventure with excellent animation ...

D
The battle scenes are breathtaking ...

E
One of the funniest movies you've ever seen!

F
The heartbreaking story of a young couple who are separated by war ...

b. How do these types of films make you react? Use the prompts to write sentences as in the example.

• laugh • cry • scream • tremble • smile
• fall asleep • sing along • bite my nails

Comedies make me laugh.

68

c. Write your TOP 5 favourite films. Make sentences, as in the example.

My favourite comedy is Austin Powers: Goldmember.

TV programmes

4 Match column A with column B to form collocations. Then, write definitions for these different kinds of TV programmes as in the example. Use your dictionary.

A	B
quiz	series
situation	show
soap	report
chat	opera
drama	comedy
news	show

A quiz show is a show in which the players answer questions and win prizes.

Newspapers and books

5 a. What is each person reading? Match the prompts with the bubbles.

- world news • detective story • biography
- review • humorous novel

1 North Korea – crops hit by heavy rains …

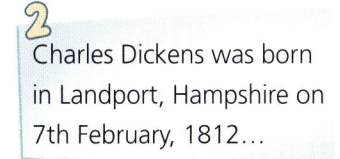

2 Charles Dickens was born in Landport, Hampshire on 7th February, 1812…

3
– Have you ever had days when you just can't get anything done?
– Days no, decades yes!

4 'Toy Story' is one of the funniest animation films ever made…

5 "This is indeed a mystery," I remarked. "What do you think it means?"

b. Which of the above pieces of writing can you find in a newspaper?

Word building

6 Use *-ive*, *–ous*, *–able*, to form adjectives from the following words. Then, use them to fill in the gaps.

fame	....	humour	....
adventure	....	collect	....
enjoy	....	memory	....
protect	....	inform	....
talk	....	express	....
admire	....	danger	....

1 Sherlock Holmes is probably the most .... detective in literature.
2 That clown has a very .... face.
3 Tom is quiet, but John is quite ....
4 'MAD' is a(n) .... magazine that makes you laugh your head off!

Prepositional phrases

7 Study the box. Then, fill in the gaps with the correct phrase.

> If something is **on your mind**, you are worried or concerned about it.
> If you ask someone what they **have in mind**, you want to know more details about an idea they have.
> If you say that someone is **out of their mind**, you mean that they are mad or very foolish.

1 What are you doing? Are you .... ?
2 This meeting has been .... all week.
3 'Let's go out tonight!' 'That's a great idea. What do you .... ?

Words often confused

8 Match the words to their definitions. Then, use them to complete the sentences.

- viewers • audience • spectators

A *a group of people watching or listening to a concert/play/film*
B *the people who watch sth live, especially a sporting event*
C *the people who watch television*

1 The .... started applauding the actors enthusiastically.
2 Millions of .... watch 'Friends' every week.
3 20,000 .... were in the stadium for the semi-final.

69

9

Grammar in use

Exploring Grammar: Conditionals

1 Read the extract from a radio interview and answer the questions below.

Interviewer: So, Jake, tell us how you became a famous pop star.
Jake: Well, it all began when I broke my leg playing football.
Interviewer: I don't understand!
Jake: It's simple. *If I hadn't broken my leg, I wouldn't have taken guitar lessons and if I hadn't learned how to play the guitar, I wouldn't have joined a band.*
Interviewer: So you owe your fame and fortune to a football injury!
Jake: Oh no, if I weren't a pop star, I'd be a famous football player!

1 Look at the sentence in italics. How many conditionals can you see? What type are they? When is this type used?
2 Look at the last sentence in the dialogue. What type of conditional sentence is it? When is this type used?
3 Which conditionals are not in the text? When are they used?

2 a. Rewrite the following sentences, using the 2nd or 3rd conditionals, as in the example.

1 She studied hard and so she graduated.
She wouldn't have graduated if she hadn't studied hard.
2 He got a promotion so he bought a car.
If he ....
....
3 She can't buy a new jumper because she doesn't have enough money.
If she ....
....
4 John isn't going on holiday as he hasn't got a job.
If John ....
....

b. Complete the sentences using the 2nd or 3rd conditional.

1 If I had more free time, ...
2 .... I would have bought him a present.
3 If I lived in Hawaii, ...
4 ...., we could have gone swimming.
5 If we had bought a new TV, ...
....

Wish/If only

3 a. Match the captions 1-4 to the pictures A-D. Then, rewrite the statements as wishes.

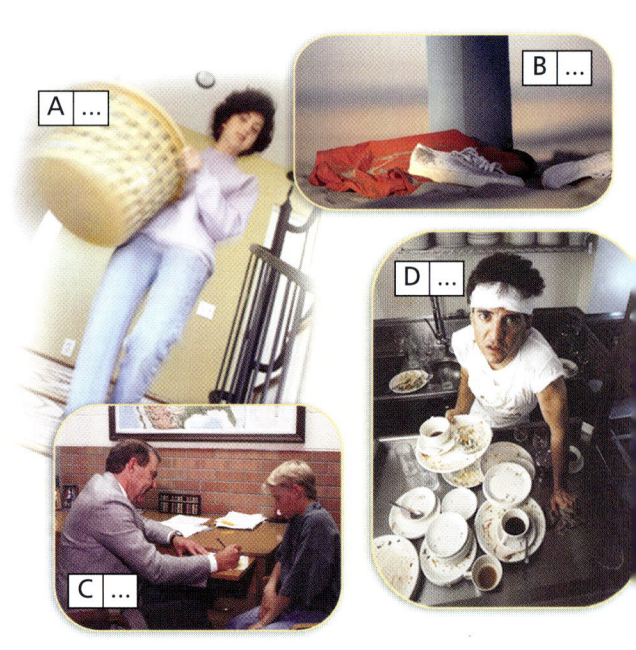

1 *"I'm sorry I cheated in my English test."*
I wish I hadn't cheated in my English test.
2 *"I'd rather be walking in the park."*
If only ....
3 *"I need to find a better job".*
If only ....
4 *"Oh no, I left my shoes and shirt on the beach!"*
I wish ....

b. Which sentences show:

A wish/regret about the past.
B wish/regret about the present.
C wish for a present/future change.

c. Complete the sentences about yourself.

1 I wish I could ....
2 I wish I hadn't ....
3 I wish I were/was ....

70

4 Look at the pictures and the speech bubbles. Use your own ideas to make sentences, as in the example.

A — I didn't bring my glasses.

She wishes she had brought her glasses. If she had brought her glasses, she would be able to read her notes.

B — I didn't take an umbrella with me.

C — I didn't read the map earlier.

D — I drank too many cold drinks.

Relative clauses

5 Use *who*, *which*, *whose* and *where* to join the following sentences.

MOVIE TRIVIA

Bruce Willis has starred in many adventure films. He was born in 1955.

....

Mary Poppins came out in 1964. It is a classic musical.

....

The Highlands are in Scotland. *Rob Roy* was shot there.

....

Michael Douglas's father is an actor. He starred in *A Perfect Murder*.

....

Phrasal verbs: turn

6 Underline the correct particle to complete the phrasal verbs.

1 At first he seemed nice, but he turned **out/up** to be a very selfish person.
2 Her constant lying really turned me **off/down** wanting to talk to her.
3 She called Laura as she had no other friend to turn **to/on**.
4 Everyone was surprised when the usually friendly dog turned **to/on** the visitor.
5 Samantha's cat disappeared only to turn **to/up** at her house four days later.
6 Bob was very upset when his girlfriend turned **off/down** his marriage proposal.

Sentence transformations

7 Rewrite the following sentences without changing the meaning.

Bookworm.com
Do you love books? Post a message on our online GUESTBOOK!

1 What we have in common is our love of literature.
   We are a group of people ....
   .... in common.
2 People don't have enough free time to read more books.
   If people had more free time, ...
   .... more books.
3 It would be great if there were more websites like this one!
   I .... more websites like this one!
4 When I was young, there weren't many websites that encouraged reading.
   If only .... more websites that encouraged reading when I was young!
5 I wanted to post a message sooner but I didn't know you had an online guest book!
   If .... you had an online guest book, I would have posted a message sooner!

9

Reading

1 a. Look at the pictures, the title and the first sentence of the article. What do you expect to read about?

b. Read the text and choose the correct answer **A**, **B**, **C** or **D**.

1 What's the writer's purpose in writing the text?
- A to make us believe that Donald is a real person
- B to embarrass his friends
- C to help Donald's acting career
- D to give us more information about Donald

2 How does the writer feel about Donald?
- A He wants to be famous like him.
- B He thinks Donald is talented, entertaining and lovable.
- C He thinks Donald is very intelligent.
- D He believes only children should like Donald.

3 Why is the writer sad that Donald won one Oscar?
- A because Donald is only a cartoon character
- B because Donald only appeared in one good cartoon
- C because he feels that Donald should have won more Oscars
- D because Donald's name was hardly ever on the list of Oscar nominees

4 The writer is trying to find facts about
- A Donald's family.
- B Donald's habits.
- C Donald's lifestyle.
- D Donald's friends.

5 Which of the following statements about Donald Duck might the writer agree with?
- A Only children like him.
- B He was funny 50 years ago.
- C He's just a drawing.
- D He is a great entertainer.

Duck Tales

I am a devoted Donald Duck fan and although my friends find it ridiculous that someone over the age of 10 has a cartoon duck for a hero, I am not ashamed. Donald is no ordinary duck. He is known throughout the world and his comics and cartoons have been translated into almost every language. I'm sure there really aren't too many people on earth who haven't heard of the world's most famous duck.

It all began in 1934 when he appeared in the Walt Disney cartoon *The Wise Little Hen*. He had a small part, but his unique voice (created by Clarence 'Duckie' Nash) and character made him a star almost overnight. He then played in many Mickey Mouse cartoons and in 1937 he finally got what he deserved: the starring role in his own cartoon called *Donald's Ostrich*. His performances were so impressive that he was often on the list of Oscar nominees, but sadly he only received one, which I feel is a shame.

There is not much information available about his personal life but here is what I've managed to find out so far. Donald was bought up by his grandmother and his rich uncle Scrooge McDuck. He has three nephews Huey, Louie and Dewey and a cousin Gus, a goose. He also has a distant European uncle called Ludwig Van Drake. I can't seem to find any information about his parents or any brothers or sisters, but I'll keep looking!

The Donald we all know and love hasn't changed much in 80 years. He's still the quick-tempered, lovable duck with that characteristic voice. What amazes me is that despite his fame and fortune, he still doesn't own one pair of trousers!

2 a. Read the text again and underline the synonyms for the following:

1 silly (para. 1)
2 embarrassed (para. 1)
3 role (para. 2)
4 wealthy (para. 3)
5 surprises (para. 4)

b. Write a short paragraph about your favourite cartoon character or comic strip hero.

Listening & Speaking

Reviewing a book

1 a. Describe the book cover. Think about:
- what the title is
- who the author is
- what type of novel this is
- what the profession of the man on the cover is
- how interesting you think it might be

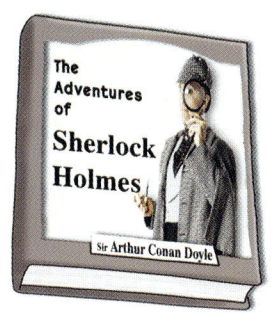

b. What is your favourite book? Write a short review of it.

Films

2 a. Read the first exchange in the dialogue. How did Bob like the film? Read the dialogue and see what reasons he gives.

b. Read the dialogue and find any phrases the speakers use to:
- correct themselves
- gain time in order to express themselves better

Then, put them in the correct category in the table.

Al: What did you think about the movie?
Bob: Well ... how shall I put it? It's 'Jaws' but ... on land and with huge spiders!
Al: Really? So you didn't like it at all! .Sorry, I shouldn't have asked you to join me.
Bob: Wait, that's not exactly what I meant to say! Let me start again! I enjoyed it but, you know, I think that this type of movie has been done many times before.
Al: Oh ... I thought that it was quite original. The special effects were impressive and the spiders were so, what's the word for it, so...life-like!
Bob: Well you have a point, Al. Hey, my friend Marco has a pet tarantula. Do you want to go and pay him a visit?
Al: I'll pass, I think I've seen enough spiders to last me a lifetime!

Conversation techniques

Hesitating	Correcting oneself
....	No .../Sorry .../I mean ...
... now let me think ...	....
... just a moment ...	....
....	... or rather ...
....	That is to say ...

c. In pairs act out similar dialogues.

Reviewing a TV programme

3 🎧 You will hear someone reviewing tonight's television programmes. For each question choose the correct answer, *A*, *B* or *C*.

1 This week, Malcolm
  A is out of town.
  B has a fight with Lois.
  C has a fight with Hal.

2 *Get a New Life* is
  A usually shown earlier.
  B usually shown later.
  C usually shown at this time.

3 *Massive Nature*
  A is a drama series.
  B is a fishing programme.
  C has won an award.

4 What time is the news on?
  A before the war film
  B after the war film
  C at 10pm

5 In *Meet the Parents*,
  A Greg's girlfriend has a difficult dad.
  B Greg's girlfriend is very pretty.
  C Greg's girlfriend is away for the weekend.

6 The presenter will return tomorrow
  A at an earlier time.
  B before the cricket match.
  C 30 minutes later.

4 What's on TV tonight? What would you like to see? Why?

9

Writing (an email of apology)

Let's get started

1 a. In which cases would someone write a letter of apology?

b. Read the rubric and underline the key words.

- A friend of yours had bought tickets for a film you both wanted to see. However, you failed to turn up. Write an email to him/her. In your email, you should:
  - apologise for not turning up
  - explain what the reason was
  - suggest a way to make it up to him/her

Let's look closer

2 a. Read the email and complete the paragraph plan. Then, answer the questions.
  – What reasons does Jenny give for her mistake?
  – How does she promise to make it up to her friend?

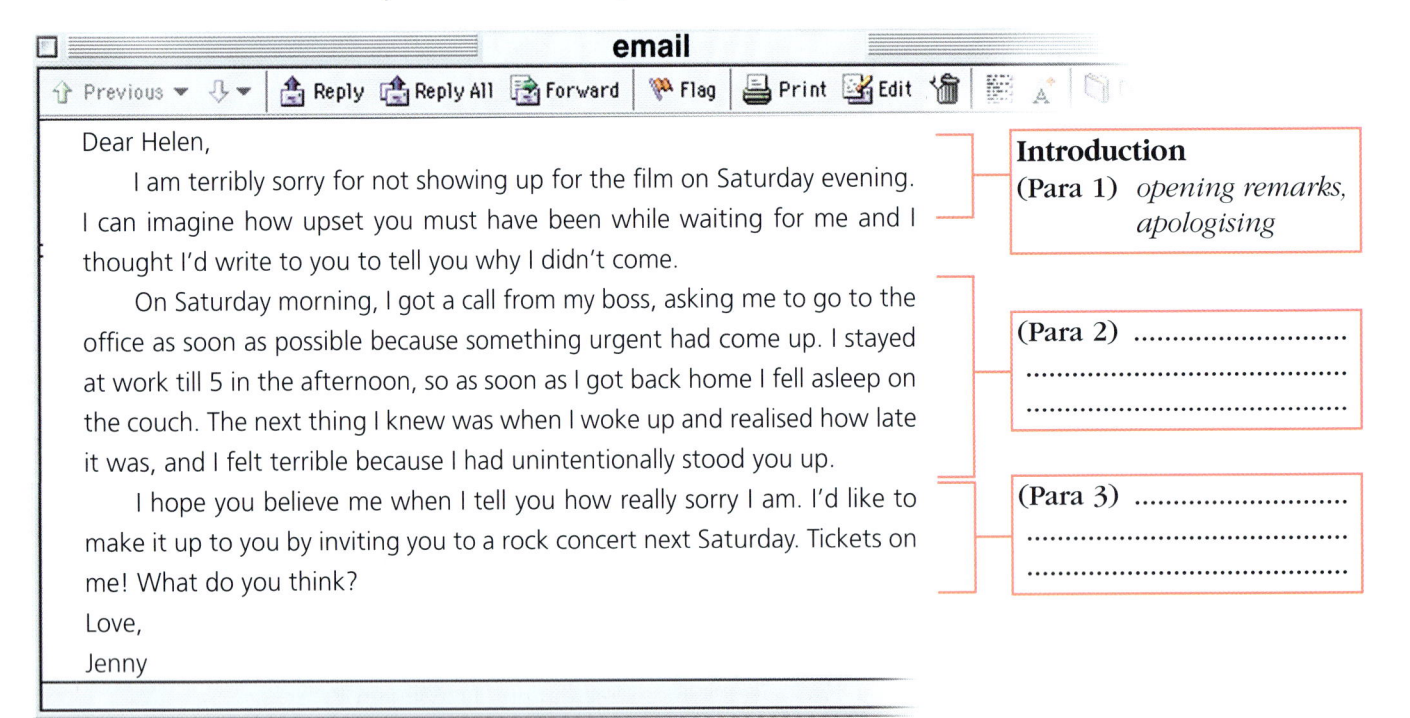

email

Dear Helen,

   I am terribly sorry for not showing up for the film on Saturday evening. I can imagine how upset you must have been while waiting for me and I thought I'd write to you to tell you why I didn't come.

   On Saturday morning, I got a call from my boss, asking me to go to the office as soon as possible because something urgent had come up. I stayed at work till 5 in the afternoon, so as soon as I got back home I fell asleep on the couch. The next thing I knew was when I woke up and realised how late it was, and I felt terrible because I had unintentionally stood you up.

   I hope you believe me when I tell you how really sorry I am. I'd like to make it up to you by inviting you to a rock concert next Saturday. Tickets on me! What do you think?

Love,
Jenny

Introduction
(Para 1) *opening remarks, apologising*

(Para 2) ....
....
....

(Para 3) ....
....
....

b. Read the email again and
- underline the expressions Jenny uses to say she is sorry
- circle the expression that means: 'to explain what happened'

Reason/Result

3 a. Look at the email again and underline any sentences that contain *because* and *so*. What do these words show?

b. Rewrite the following sentences as in the example.

1 He helped me. I didn't know how to do it.
   He helped me because I didn't know how to do it.
   I didn't know how to do it, so he helped me.

2 I called you. I wanted to apologise.
3 Tina started crying. She was very disappointed.
4 We will give you a refund. The product is faulty.

Making excuses

4 Write sentences excusing yourself in the following situations.

1 You forgot your best friend's birthday.
I'm sorry I forgot your birthday, but I had been ill in hospital.

2 You missed your cousin's wedding.
The reason I .... was .... I'm deeply sorry.

3 You didn't turn up for a very important meeting at work.
I apologise for .... What happened was ....

4 You damaged a friend's CD player.
I feel so guilty about ....
What happened was ....

5 You spoke rudely to a friend.
Please forgive me for ....
At that moment, I felt ....

Making it up

5 a. Write sentences suggesting ways to make it up to the following people.

1 You lost a book a friend had given you.
I'm sorry I lost your book. I will buy you another one.

2 You damaged a friend's camera.
....
....

3 You weren't able to go to your friend's birthday party.
....
....

4 You forgot a meeting with a friend.
How does ....
....

b. Think of other ideas for Jenny to make it up to Helen in Ex. 2.

Your turn

6 a. Read the rubric and underline the key words. Then, use expressions from the useful language box to make your points.

You missed your best friend's birthday party. Write an email to him/her to say you are sorry. In your email, you should:
- apologise for having missed the event
- justify yourself
- suggest a way to make it up to him/her

Useful language

Making excuses
- I'm sorry ...
- The reason I ...
- I do apologise for ...
- I feel so guilty ...
- Please forgive me for ...

Making it up
- Please let me ... to make it up to you.
- I promise I'll ...
- I'd like to make it up to you by ...

b. Look at the opening/closing remarks below and mark the sentences *(F)* for formal and *(I)* for informal. Which ones would you choose to start/end your email?

Opening remarks
- I am writing to apologise for ...
- I'm sorry for ...
- Please accept my sincere apologies for ...
- I can't tell you how sorry I am ...
- I owe you an apology for ...

Closing remarks
- I hope you will accept my apologies for ...
- There's no excuse for ... and I hope you'll forgive me for ...
- I beg you to forgive me for ...

c. Now, write your email (60-100 words).

Fast Forward

Vocabulary Practice

Technology

1 a. Label the devices Terence has in his room. Use the phrases in the box to say what each one is used for.

- listen to music
- make paper copies
- take pictures
- watch programmes
- play music
- record/amplify your voice
- store information

A printer is used to make paper copies of documents.

b. Which of the above devices have/haven't you got in your room?

2 a. Name two devices that have the following features.

1	cables	*computer, camera*
2	voice recorder	....
3	screen	....
4	headphones	....
5	colour monitor	....
6	hard disk	....
7	microphone	....

Problems

b. Use the prompts in the box to write sentences, as in the example.

- I've been having problems with ... .
- I can't get it to start.
- It keeps crashing/turning black/jumping/flickering/getting stuck
- It won't come on.
- The ... doesn't work.

I've been having problems with my computer. It keeps crashing.

3 Fill in: *from, onto, on, to, with, down, at*.

1 Where did you find this song? I downloaded it .... the Internet .... my computer.
2 In her free time, she chats with her friends .... the net and she plays games .... her computer.
3 Did you take these lovely pictures .... your digital camera?
4 He types all his essays .... his laptop.
5 She used a modem to connect the computer .... the phone line.
6 The information he wanted wasn't .... the top of the webpage, so he scrolled .... to find it.

4 Use the prompts to respond.

- turn down • plug in • switch off
- log on • delete

1 A: The music is too loud!
　B: *OK. I'll turn it down!*
2 A: The TV is annoying me!
　B: ....
3 A: The computer doesn't work.
　B: ....
4 A: This file is useless!
　B: ....
5 A: I want to use the Internet!
　B: ....

10

Wordsearch puzzle

5 Unscramble the nouns defined below. Then, find them in the wordsearch puzzle.

1 A device you type on to input information into a computer. (darobeky) *keyboard*
2 An electronic letter or message you send over the Internet. (meila) ....
3 The part of a desk top computer where the screen is located. (omitron) ....
4 The secret code word you use to log on to your computer. (droswasp) ....
5 A collection of Internet files on a particular subject, with its own homepage. (tisbewe) ....
6 A device used to point at and select options on a computer screen. (Hint: It's named after a small animal.) (smeou) ....
7 A machine that makes a paper copy of a text, picture, etc from your computer. (tirnerp) ....

```
E M O N W O A R B S
M O U S E P R Y M O
A N D S B A O M P U
I S P A S S W O R D
L A R W I U E N E Y
O D I E T L B I L I
P I N R E T S T E R
A S T E R Y C O L P
L K E Y B O A R D N
D I R S T U M C O E
```

Education

6 What kind of modern equipment can you use in each class? Use the prompts and your own ideas to make sentences.

- digital camera • overhead projector
- video recorder • desktop computer

An overhead projector can be used in science lessons to show slides of body parts.

art class   science class
astronomy class   computer class

Word formation: prefixes

7 Study the box and form verbs. Then, use them to complete the sentences (1-4).

re- is added to verbs and nouns to form new verbs and nouns that refer to the repeating of an action or a process.

inter- combines with verbs and nouns to form adjectives indicating that something connects two or more places, things or groups of people.

change ....   start ....
appear ....   national ....
charge ....   arrange ....

1 British Airways is offering a discount on .... flights this month!
2 My battery is low. I have to .... my phone.
3 The teacher .... the desks to make space for the meeting.
4 I thought I'd lost my files, but they .... when I restarted my computer.

Prepositional phrases

8 Study the box, then complete the sentences 1-4 with the right phrase.

> If something is in sight, you can see it.
> If something is out of sight, you cannot see it.
> If you know someone by sight, you can recognise them when you see them, although you have never met or talked to them.
> If you say that something has certain characteristics at first sight, you mean that it appears to have the features you describe when you first see it but later it is found to be different.

1 As the boat neared the island, the small beach was ....
2 The project seemed more difficult ....
3 I've never spoken to Julian, but I know him ....
4 He parked his car .... so that nobody would know he was home.

77

10

Grammar in Use

Exploring Grammar: Indirect speech

1 Read the speech bubbles, then read the dialogue and answer the questions.

Technical Support? You've got to help me! My computer's cupholder is broken!

It's like a tray that comes out of the front of my PC, with a hole in it for my coffee cup.

Hmm, we don't normally deal with things like that. Can you describe it to me?

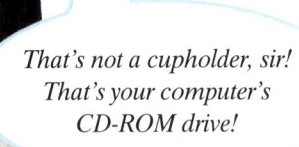

That's not a cupholder, sir! That's your computer's CD-ROM drive!

Kelly: Someone called our Help Desk today and said that his cupholder was broken!

James: What does a cupholder have to do with Computer Technical Support?

Kelly: Exactly! I asked him to describe it to me. In the end I told him it was his CD-ROM drive!

1 Which sentences from the speech bubbles are reported in the dialogue? Compare them with the ones in the speech bubbles. How have the verb tenses changed? Why have they changed?

2 Look at the direct question in italics in the speech bubbles and then find the reported question in the dialogue. What are the changes that take place when reporting direct questions?

3 Apart from the verb tenses, what else changes when reporting another person's words?

2 Read the note John found from his mum when he got home from school.

> I've gone to visit Mrs Patterson. I'll be back at 10:00pm. Order pizza for dinner. Call me on my mobile if you need me.
> Love,
> Mum

Complete the text to report what John's mother said in her note.

> John's mum left him a note which said that she had gone ...

3 You have a foreign exchange student in your class and she has asked you a lot of questions. You are telling your friend what she said.

> She asked me where the headmaster's office was, what we had to wear for PE, what type of food they served in the cafeteria and what time the school bus picked us up after school.

Rewrite her questions as direct questions.

1 *Where is the headmaster's office?*
2 ....
3 ....
4 ....

4 a. Complete the speech bubbles with the correct forms of the reporting verbs below.

• tell • say • ask

1
"You must eat properly and get eight hour's sleep each night", the doctor .... her.

2
"What is Todd doing tonight?" Ann .... Jane.

3
"I'm going to Japan for Christmas," Judy ....

78

b. Report what was said in the speech bubbles.

1 The doctor told her ....
2 Ann asked ....
3 Judy said ....

5 Report the following orders:

1 "Stop talking or I'll give you extra homework."
 The teacher told us ....
2 "Clara, switch the radio off!"
 Mum told Clara ....
3 "Don't delete these files!"
 My boss told me ....

Causative form

6 **a.** Your friend is having problems with his computer and asks for your advice. Complete the dialogue, using the causative form.

1 A: My disk drive won't read my floppy disks. (fix)
 B: *You should have it fixed.*
2 A: My monitor keeps going black.
 B: .... (check by technician)
3 A: There's no sound coming from my speakers.
 B: .... (replace)
4 A: The keys on my keyboard keep sticking.
 B: .... (clean)

b. Your friend's TV has broken and his video is not working. Write the dialogues.

1 A: ....
 B: ....

2 A: ....
 B: ....

10

Phrasal verbs: take

7 Choose the correct particle.

1 A: She has been taking **on/up** far too much work lately. She needs to slow down.
 B: I know. I've told her so myself.
2 A: Where are William and Sam?
 B: They took **off/out** for the weekend.
3 A: Fred's new computer system takes **up/on** half the space in his bedroom.
 B: Yes, I know. Have you seen all the equipment he got with it?
4 A: Jimmy seems to have a lot of money, doesn't he?
 B: I know! He took all his friends **out/up** to dinner at the weekend.

Sentence transformations

8 Complete the second sentence so that it means the same as the first. Use no more than three words.

1 "Why has Mary deleted all her files?" he wondered.
 He wondered why .... all her files.
2 Someone is coming to repair the photocopier this afternoon.
 We are .... repaired this afternoon.
3 Two thieves entered my house and stole everything.
 Two thieves broke .... and stole everything.
4 "Where is my laptop?" Ron asked his sister.
 Ron asked his sister ....
 .... was.
5 "The technician will be here in an hour," the secretary said.
 The secretary said that the technician ....
 .... in an hour.

79

10

Reading

1 Which of the sentences below do you think are true about the girl in the picture? Decide, then read the text and check your guesses.

1 She gets up early.
2 Her school is traditional and old fashioned.
3 She studies hard.
4 She uses lots of gadgets and appliances.
5 She doesn't often go out during the week.

2 Read the text again and choose the best answer *A*, *B*, *C* or *D*.

1 In this text, Atsuko describes
   A her typical weekend.
   B her daily routine.
   C how technology has changed her life.
   D Japanese traditions.

2 After she wakes up, Atsuko
   A gets out of bed and listens to the news.
   B gets up and reads the news.
   C has breakfast and goes to school.
   D gets up and takes the bus to school.

3 On the way to school, children don't
   A listen to music.
   B talk to their friends.
   C do their homework.
   D watch TV.

4 What does Atsuko say about school work?
   A She complains that the teachers give her bad grades.
   B She says that she would get better results with a new PC.
   C She would rather talk to her friends than study.
   D She says her parents help her with her studies.

5 What might Atsuko say about her life?
   A I wish I could spend all day in my room listening to music.
   B If I had more time, I would read lots of books.
   C I study quite hard, so I really look forward to the weekends.
   D I would get better school grades if I didn't chat so much on my mobile!

A Day in the Life of a Japanese Teen

15-year-old Atsuko Kawabata tells Teen World how technology plays a major role in her daily life.

6.30am My alarm clock goes off and I get out of bed and turn on my stereo to catch up on the news.

7.30am Time to put on my headphones and go to school with music blasting from my personal stereo.

7.45am As soon as I get onto the school bus, I swap CDs with my friends. Some of them are finishing up their homework on their laptops. Others are gossiping with their friends on their mobiles. Younger passengers are having fun with their Gameboys.

8.30am In the classroom, which is equipped with state-of-the-art PCs, I do my best to concentrate on my Maths lesson. Some kids download games from the Internet, while pretending to work hard on Maths problems.

6.00pm Home at last! At the dinner table, I complain about the homework my teachers give me. Lately, I've been trying to convince my parents that a new and better computer would help me to improve my grades at school. Then I do my homework. While doing it, I have to have my mobile switched off. When I've finished, I turn on my mobile and start chatting to my friends. Sometimes I go out to a café, but I am not usually allowed to go out until the weekend. That's when I have the most fun!

3 a. Read the text again and underline all the things related to modern technology that Atsuko uses.

  b. Write sentences about the gadgets that you use every day.

  I use an alarm clock to wake me up in the morning.

Listening & Speaking

Making a phone call

1 Use the verbs below to complete the instructions.

• insert • make • hold • dial

1 .... your card.

2 .... the number.

3 .... a phonecall.

4 .... the line.

2 a. Listen and fill in the missing information.

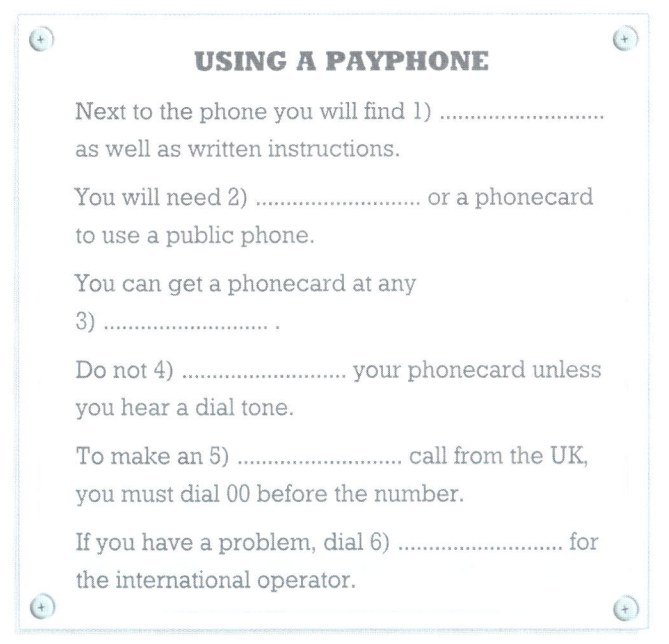

USING A PAYPHONE

Next to the phone you will find 1) .... as well as written instructions.

You will need 2) .... or a phonecard to use a public phone.

You can get a phonecard at any 3) ....

Do not 4) .... your phonecard unless you hear a dial tone.

To make an 5) .... call from the UK, you must dial 00 before the number.

If you have a problem, dial 6) .... for the international operator.

b. How do you make a phone call in your country? Give instructions to a foreigner.

Talking on the phone

3 a. Read the first lines of the dialogues (A + B). What is the relationship between the speakers?

A

Mona: Hello. Is Tim there, please?
Bob: Is that you, Mona?
Mona: Yes ... Oh, hi, Bob! I didn't recognise your voice.
Bob: Hi, Mona. Well, Tim is in the bathroom right now. Can you hold the line?
Mona: I think I'll call back later. Bye!

B

A: Smith, Harper and Jarvis Enterprises – can I help you?
B: Good morning. Could you put me through to Mr. Smith, please?
A: May I ask who's calling?
B: This is Mrs Bell, the accountant.
A: I'm afraid he's not here right now. He'll be back this afternoon.
B: Oh no! This afternoon is too late. What about Mr. Harper? Is he there?
A: Yes, but I'm afraid he can't come to the phone right now. He's in an important meeting. Can I take a message?
B: Oh, no, that's all right. Can I speak to Mr. Jarvis instead, please?
A: Certainly. I'll put you through to him.

b. Find and underline phrases in the dialogues that the speakers use to ask for someone.

c. How do you answer the phone in your own language? Is it the same as in English?

4 Read the phrases in the box and mark them **(F)** for formal, **(I)** for informal or **(B)** for both. Then, act out a short dialogue similar to A.

Speaker A - Asking

Could I speak to ... , please?   ....
Is that ...?   ....
Could I leave a message?   ....
Could you ask him to call back?   ....
Could you tell him that ... called?   ....

Speaker B - Responding

... speaking – may I help you?   ....
Would you like to leave a message?   ....
Yes, speaking.   ....
Can you ring back later?   ....
Who is it?   ....
Will you hold?   ....

81

10

Writing (a letter requesting information)

Getting started

1 Read the rubric and underline the key words. Is this a formal or an informal letter? How will you start and end it?

- Read the advertisement for a local computer club you want to join, and the notes you have made. Then, write a letter to the club secretary asking for information, including the points mentioned in your notes.

WE'RE OPEN

Ashton Computer Club is now open with brand new facilities!
30 PCs all with broadband Internet connection

how much membership cost?

what is free gift?

- Become a member with free entry for one year and get a FREE GIFT!
All ages and abilities welcome!

separate groups for kids/adults?

6, Lockfield Road, Ashton
10am – 10pm, every day

Let's look closer

2 a. Read the letter and complete the paragraph plan.

Dear Sir/Madam,

1▶ I saw your advertisement in the Ashton Gazette yesterday and I am interested in becoming a member of the computer club. However, I would appreciate it if you could give me some more information.

2▶ First of all, could you please let me know how much membership costs? I would also like to know what the free gift mentioned in your advertisement is.

3▶ Secondly, I would like to know whether there will be separate classes for children and adults.

4▶ Thank you in advance for your help. I look forward to hearing from you as soon as possible.

Yours faithfully,
Darren Brown

Introduction
(Para 1) *Reason for writing*

(Para 2) ....
....
....

(Para 3) ....
....
....

Conclusion
(Para 4) *Closing remarks*

b. Read the letter again and underline the phrases Darren uses to ask for information. How many direct questions can you find in the letter?

c. What is the first thing Darren mentions in the introduction?

Requesting information

3 a. Use the phrases in the box below to turn the direct questions into indirect questions.

Indirect Questions

- Could you let me know/tell me …
- I would like to know (if/whether) …
- I would like you to tell me …
- Can you explain what you mean by …
- I am also interested in finding out …
---

1 Are the computer instructors qualified?
2 Are there any laptops for hire at the club?
3 What software do the computers have?
4 Is there air conditioning in the rooms?
5 How close is the club to the university campus?
6 Does membership include the use of all the facilities?

b. Look at the advert in Ex. 1 again and think of other indirect questions you could ask about the computer club.

Opening/Closing remarks

4 Which of the following are opening remarks and which are closing remarks? Mark them *(O)* for opening and *(C)* for closing.

1 I am writing to ask for some information about the adventure weekend I saw advertised in this week's edition of *Adventure Lovers*.
2 I look forward to hearing from you soon.
3 Please write back soon with the information.
4 I saw your advert in *Keyboard* magazine and I want to know more.

Your turn

5 a. You are interested in joining a photography club. Use the prompts in the box to ask the secretary for information.

- opening and closing times • classes
- qualified instructors • student discount

I would like to know if there is a special discount for students at your club.

b. Read the rubric below and underline the key words. Then, use your ideas in Ex. 5a and the expressions from Ex. 3a to write your letter (100-120 words).

Read the advert for a local photography club you want to join, and the notes you have made. Then write a letter to the secretary of the photography club, asking for information including the points mentioned in your notes.

PHOTOGRAPHER'S WORLD
Bolton PHOTOGRAPHY CLUB

The members of Bolton Photography Club invite you to join our club and enjoy all the various activities relating to photography. The Club meets on the second Monday of each month at 6:30 at the Local Library. Brand new facilities. All ages and levels of experience welcome!

Is there a membership fee? How much?

What kind of activities?

Equipment provided or do we have to bring our own?

83

Irregular Verbs

Infinitive	Past	Past Participle	Infinitive	Past	Past Participle
be	was	been	lie	lay	lain
bear	bore	born(e)	light	lit	lit
beat	beat	beaten	lose	lost	lost
become	became	become	make	made	made
begin	began	begun	mean	meant	meant
bite	bit	bitten	meet	met	met
blow	blew	blown	pay	paid	paid
break	broke	broken	put	put	put
bring	brought	brought	read	read	read
build	built	built	ride	rode	ridden
burn	burnt (burned)	burnt (burned)	ring	rang	rung
burst	burst	burst	rise	rose	risen
buy	bought	bought	run	ran	run
can	could	(been able to)	say	said	said
catch	caught	caught	see	saw	seen
choose	chose	chosen	seek	sought	sought
come	came	come	sell	sold	sold
cost	cost	cost	send	sent	sent
cut	cut	cut	set	set	set
deal	dealt	dealt	sew	sewed	sewn
dig	dug	dug	shake	shook	shaken
do	did	done	shine	shone	shone
dream	dreamt (dreamed)	dreamt (dreamed)	shoot	shot	shot
drink	drank	drunk	show	showed	shown
drive	drove	driven	shut	shut	shut
eat	ate	eaten	sing	sang	sung
fall	fell	fallen	sit	sat	sat
feed	fed	fed	sleep	slept	slept
feel	felt	felt	smell	smelt (smelled)	smelt (smelled)
fight	fought	fought	speak	spoke	spoken
find	found	found	spell	spelt (spelled)	spelt (spelled)
flee	fled	fled	spend	spent	spent
fly	flew	flown	split	split	split
forbid	forbade	forbidden	spread	spread	spread
forget	forgot	forgotten	spring	sprang	sprung
forgive	forgave	forgiven	stand	stood	stood
freeze	froze	frozen	steal	stole	stolen
get	got	got	stick	stuck	stuck
give	gave	given	sting	stung	stung
go	went	gone	stink	stank	stunk
grow	grew	grown	strike	struck	struck
hang	hung (hanged)	hung (hanged)	swear	swore	sworn
have	had	had	sweep	swept	swept
hear	heard	heard	swim	swam	swum
hide	hid	hidden	take	took	taken
hit	hit	hit	teach	taught	taught
hold	held	held	tear	tore	torn
hurt	hurt	hurt	tell	told	told
keep	kept	kept	think	thought	thought
know	knew	known	throw	threw	thrown
lay	laid	laid	understand	understood	understood
lead	led	led	wake	woke	woken
learn	learnt (learned)	learnt (learned)	wear	wore	worn
leave	left	left	win	won	won
lend	lent	lent	write	wrote	written
let	let	let			

Tapescripts

UNIT 1

◆ Tapescript for Exercise 1 (p. 9)

Presenter: …which brings us to our next subject for today – body language. And with us to talk about this fascinating topic is the well-known psychologist Dr Sue Williams. Thank you for coming.

Dr Williams: It's my pleasure.

Presenter: Well, doctor Williams. Could you tell us exactly what body language is?

Dr Williams: Basically, it is communication using the body instead of words. For example, take a look at how we are sitting right now. You will notice that our bodies and our knees are pointing towards one another. When people sit this way it usually means they are interested and feel comfortable with the person facing them. This is an example of body language, or non-verbal communication.

Presenter: And is this form of communication of any importance to us?

Dr Williams: Certainly! A lot can be understood from someone's body language. I am sure you will agree that people sometimes say quite the opposite to what they really feel. But the body doesn't lie and reveals the truth about how someone feels. So a good observer can get a lot of information about someone from their body language.

Presenter: Oh! I'll have to be careful in future. Tell me more. How does the body speak, then?

Dr Williams: In a number of ways. The way we move our hands, the position of parts of our bodies such as our knees, as I have already mentioned, and of course the movement of our eyes, give away a lot of information about us. Some people, for instance, don't like to stand too close to the person they are talking to because it makes them feel very uncomfortable. Others consider this to be a way of showing interest in the person or a way of expressing a sense of closeness or friendship.

Presenter: And is body language the same for everybody, or does it vary from culture to culture?

Dr Williams: Yes, body language depends a lot on culture. A few facial expressions and gestures may be common to all but in general, people of different cultures tend to have very different ways of expressing themselves. In some countries, for instance, it is necessary to look into the eyes of the person you are talking to in order to show interest in what he or she is saying, while in other countries, it is rude or insulting to look into someone's eyes. Also, in some countries, nodding your head expresses agreement while in others this would mean that you disagree.

Presenter: That's odd, isn't it? Imagine not knowing if someone agrees with you or not. How about women and men – any differences?

Dr Williams: Oh yes. According to recent research, women use body language more than men.

Presenter: Well, that seems reasonable to me. Let's take a short commercial break and we'll be back in a few minutes.

UNIT 2

◆ Tapescript for Exercise 5b (p. 17)

Pam: So, Greg, have you finally decided what you are going to do after university?

Greg: No, I haven't made my mind up yet. I might go travelling for a year. What about you? You've still got another, what… three years at medical school, haven't you?

Pam: Yeah, that's right – and in the meantime, I'm stuck working at Gresham's restaurant.

Greg: I thought you liked working there.

Pam: Well, the tips can be great and the customers are usually really polite and friendly, even when I get the order wrong, which is not often, but it's really tiring being on your feet all the time.

Greg: Well, I bet you're looking forward to becoming a doctor, then.

Pam: Yeah, although the salary's not great from the start. You have to wait years and pass lots of exams before you start earning a better salary.

Greg: It's not just the money, though, is it? I mean, you will be doing something really worthwhile, helping sick people get better, and the career prospects are great, aren't they?

Pam: Yeah, you're right, I suppose I'm just a bit tired after doing a late shift last night at the restaurant. I had to cover for a girl who was off sick.

Greg: Just think, though. In a few years time, you won't be getting tips from customers, you'll be able to go out to nice places and give tips.

Pam: And I'll leave big tips after having worked as a waitress. Imagine having to do that for the rest of your life.

Greg: So you don't think the career prospects are great? (laughs)

Pam: No, that's one of the reasons I'm going into medicine. What about you, Greg? You're not going to spend the rest of your life borrowing money from your parents, are you?

Greg: No way! I'm going to be a rich and famous.

Pam: You wish!

85

Tapescripts

UNIT 3

◆ **Tapescript for Exercise 3 (p. 25)**

Presenter:

Now, if everyone's ready, I'd like to talk about giving speeches and presentations. The key to doing this successfully is, of course, preparation. If you are well-prepared and know what you want to say, then you won't feel nervous. Keep your notes in front of you to look at while you are making your presentation. However, try to keep them short, clear and easy to read.

Now, a word about using videos, slide projectors and other audio/visual equipment. If you decide to use these in your presentation, especially things like microphones and amplifiers, check that they are working properly before you begin speaking. As for speaking itself, the rule is to speak louder than you think you need to. Most people talk much too quietly and nobody can hear what they're saying.

Finally, even the best speakers dry up sometimes. If this happens to you, the worst thing you can do is panic! Try to stay calm because this will help you remember what you want to say. Above all, be professional! A speech usually turns out to be bad when the speaker is shy or when his preparation is poor. On the other hand, the most successful speakers are both confident and enthusiastic. To give you an example of what I mean … (fade)

UNIT 4

◆ **Tapescript for Exercise 4b (p. 33)**

Dave: So Tracey, how was your holiday in Bournemouth?
Tracey: Well, it was good and bad, actually.
Dave: Oh, yes? I heard the weather was good though, wasn't it?
Tracey: Yes, it was, but the hotel we stayed at wasn't exactly great.
Dave: Oh dear. What was the matter with it, then?
Tracey: For a start, there was nowhere to park our car and the August traffic was terrible.
Dave: Well, August is a busy time of year.
Tracey: Yeah, well. When we arrived we were really hungry but the restaurant had closed for the evening!
Dave: Typical!
Tracey: They weren't too keen to serve us at other times, either and the service was awful and unfriendly. Plus there wasn't even any room service.
Dave: You must be joking! So you must have eaten out a lot?
Tracey: Yes. We did use the pool quite a lot though as it was quieter than the crowded beach and it was better for Jamie – who's only 18 months old, remember.
Dave: Right. I suppose there was a television in the room?
Tracey: Not only that, but lots of satellite channels and a DVD player as well.
Dave: It sounds like you spent most of your holiday watching TV!
Tracey: We did watch a bit but as you said, the weather was really hot so we sat by the swimming pool a lot. Besides, there wasn't any air conditioning in the rooms.
Dave: That's hardly a surprise. This country's not used to hot weather.
Tracey: Yeah, tell me about it. I must say, though, that the rooms were spotlessly clean, so we left the maid a good tip when we left.
Dave: That was good of you. Do you think you'll be going back?
Tracey: No, but we might have if the service had been a bit more friendly.
Dave: Right.

UNIT 5

◆ **Tapescript for Exercise 2 (p. 41)**

Samantha: Come on Bill, hurry up! We don't have much time before the shopping centre closes.
Bill: I'm coming, I just need to lock the car. Here we are.
Samantha: OK let's go. You know I'm really looking forward to Maria's wedding and I want you to look your best. All my family will be there. You can try on a few suits to see what size fits you best, eh.
Bill: Samantha, it's easy. I know my size so let's just go straight to Burton's and get a black suit like the old one I have.
Samantha: Oh I think you should get a grey one. Grey really suits you and then you could also wear it to work.
Bill: OK then, grey is fine with me, but I need to get a tie to match.
Samantha: Right. Oh just a second, look at those purple high-heels. Oh they're lovely, aren't they? They would go perfectly with my dress. Let's go inside.
Bill: I'll wait here if you don't mind.

(Pause)

Bill: What took you so long? I've been waiting for you for ages!
Samantha: Sorry, it was really busy, but they were a real bargain. They only cost £26 down from £35.
Bill: Great. Shall we go now?
Samantha: Oh look at the time! We'd better hurry up. The men's shop is over there.
Bill: Yes, and it looks like they are closing.
Samantha: Closing? Are you sure?
Bill: Well I think they've put the closed sign up. Yeah, closed.
Samantha: Oh no! You've no suit for the wedding.
Bill: That's all right. I'll just wear my old one. Come on! Let's go.

Tapescripts

UNIT 6

◆ Tapescript for Exercise 1 (p. 49)

1 How many gifts has Jim received?

Mum: Oh, what beautiful presents Aunt Mary brought for you! What have you got, Fiona?
Fiona: I've got a pink dress.
Mum: And what about you, Jim?
Jim: I've got some books ... *The Three Musketeers*, *Treasure Island* and *Robinson Crusoe*.

2 Who does Mark invite?

Mark: Shall I ask Henry's brother, David, to the party?
Woman: I think he's away on holiday. Henry's coming though, isn't he?
Mark: I'm still waiting for his reply to our invitation.
Woman: Well, send David one anyway. He may be back by now.

3 What did the couple forget?

Man: Quick, give me the camera. Sarah's about to blow out the candles on her cake.
Woman: It's here but you didn't remind me to get film!
Man: Oh dear! We could have had some great shots for the family photo album.

4 Which lantern did Rachel make?

Rachel: That isn't the one I made. Mine's got teeth and triangular eyes. The one Charlie made looks similar but it hasn't got a nose. Mine must be on the other table.

UNIT 7

◆ Tapescript for Exercise 2a (p. 57)

Answering machine: Thank you for calling Fisher's Organic Fruit and Vegetables. Please leave your message after the tone ... (beep)

Chef: Hello. This is Oliver Jones – chef at the Bay Tree Restaurant. I'm phoning about the fruit and veg you delivered yesterday because there seems to have been a mistake.

For a start, I only ordered 6 kilos of carrots, not 10 as it says on your invoice. I don't need that many. And I'm certainly not going to pay for two boxes of baby onions. You've only delivered one! Where is the other box?

The cooking apples ... yes, they're OK. Two crates for £11 which is what I wanted. But I'm sure you've overcharged me for the wild mushrooms! I know they're expensive but do you really expect me to pay £200 for 3 kilograms? That can't be right, can it? As for the lettuce, I'm sure I ordered four boxes but if you check the invoice, it says three.

The blood oranges ... let's see ... Yes, you delivered 5 kilos and that's correct. But what about the aubergines? You've charged me for 15 kilos but I haven't received any at all! You should have delivered 8 kilos and I wanted them for tonight's menu. Please call me back as soon as possible on 0131 445 5690.

UNIT 8

◆ Tapescript for Exercise 2b (p. 65)

SOC guide:

If you would like to take part in the Schools Outdoor Challenge rock climbing course, your teacher will give you an application form at the end of the lesson. For now, I'll tell you what the cost of the course includes and what you need to bring with you.

As you can see from our leaflet, rock climbing involves quite a lot of equipment, but don't worry! All the technical climbing gear – footwear, harnesses, helmets and ropes – is included in the cost of the course. Course guides and transportation, plus adult supervision during non-climbing hours are also included as well as your accommodation at the Newton Inn and all meals – but if you have any dietary restrictions, please let us know as soon as possible.

As a climber, here is what you need to bring:
Firstly, you'll need a backpack or a rucksack. You'll also need toiletries such as soap, toothpaste and so on, and a small first-aid kit with plasters, tape and bandages. This is in case you get cuts or minor injuries – although, of course, we hope you won't!

You should also bring a waterproof jacket and plenty of warm clothes, thick socks and you may want to bring some thermal underwear as evenings in the mountains can be very cold. Having said that, it can get quite hot in the daytime so you must bring sunscreen, sunglasses and something to protect your head! Climbing will also make you thirsty, so bring two water bottles. If the weather's good, you'll have the chance to go swimming in one of the lovely mountain lakes, too, so don't forget your swimsuit and a towel!

Finally, we recommend you bring about £40-£50 in pocket money for daytime snacks or evening treats back at the Inn. The application form contains a complete list of all the items you need, but for now are there any questions?

Tapescripts

UNIT 9

◆ Tapescript for Exercise 3 (p. 73)

So here's the pick of tonight's TV.

At 7:10 on BBC2 there's the sitcom *Malcolm in the Middle*. This week, while Lois is out of town, Malcolm and Hal have a fight, which ends up with Malcolm getting thrown out of his home.

Then straight after that at 8:00 pm – an earlier time than usual – you can see what happens to a family who decide to move to Sweden in *Get a New Life*. Trevor and Cathy Muir think they've found the ideal place to bring up their children in a small Swedish town, but is it too small for them to find work, even with some help?

Next, over on BBC1 at 8:30, you can see the award-winning documentary series *Massive Nature*. This week's episode is called *The Falls*. Every year 300 million salmon migrate up rivers across Alaska, but they're swimming into a trap. At waterfalls upstream, the fish are attacked by bears and bald eagles.

Tonight's film is *U-571* [2000] at 9 o'clock on Channel 4. This is a wartime action drama starring Harvey Keitel and Jon Bon Jovi. An American submarine crew are on a mission to seize an Enigma machine and manage to take over the enemy's boat. The film continues after *News at Ten*.

Or if you'd rather watch a comedy, Channel 5 is showing *Meet the Parents* [2000] at 9.45, starring Robert De Niro and Ben Stiller. Greg is about to spend his first weekend with his girlfriend's parents and he's pretty nervous about it. Although he tries very hard to please her difficult dad, his attempts result in very comic situations.

That's all from me for today. I'll be back tomorrow at the slightly later time of 6.45 so that cricket fans don't miss the last half hour of the test match.

UNIT 10

◆ Tapescript for Exercise 2a (p. 81)

Woman: OK class, we've gone over how to use the public transport system and now I'd like to make sure that you all know how to use the public telephones while you are in the UK. Their public phones are similar to ours but there are a few differences. There are written instructions next to the phone, in English of course, but there are also drawings to show you what to do.

To use a public phone you need coins, or a phonecard. I recommend you get a phonecard because these are much more convenient to use. You can buy a phonecard from any newsagent's, and I suggest you do that at the airport as soon as you arrive. To make a phone call from a public phone box do the following: First, pick up the receiver and listen for the dial tone. If there is no dial tone, that means the phone isn't working and you should find another one. When you hear the dial tone, insert your phonecard. There is a screen on the phone that will tell you how much money you have left on your card, and you can see if your phonecard is running out.

Then, just dial the number. Remember that if you are making an international call from the UK, you have to dial 00 before the number. You will also need to know the country code of the number you want to call. For us the code is 30. If you have any problems making the call, you can get through to the international operator by dialing 155.

In case of an emergency you ...